Real World Research

Observation Techniques

Also available from Continuum

Real World Research Series

Case Study Research Methods, Bill Gillham

The Research Interview, Bill Gillham

Small-scale Social Survey Methods, Bill Gillham

Developing a Questionnaire 2nd Edition, Bill Gillham

Also available

Questionnaire Design, Interviewing and Attitude Measurement, A. N. Oppenheim

Observation Techniques

Structured to Unstructured

Bill Gillham
Real World Research

continuum

Continuum International Publishing Group
The Tower Building   80 Maiden Lane, Suite 704
11 York Road   New York, NY 10038
London SE1 7NX
www.continuumbooks.com

First published 2008.

British Library Cataloguing-in-Publication Data
A catalogue record for this book is available from the British Library.

ISBN: 9780826496294 (paperback)

Library of Congress Cataloging-in-Publication Data
A catalog record for this book is available from the Library of Congress.

Typeset by YHT Ltd, London
Printed and bound in Great Britain by MPG Books Ltd, Bodmin, UK.

Contents

List of Figures and Tables   vii

Series Foreword   ix

Acknowledgements   xi

1   Why Observe?   1

2   Structured Observation   9

3   Semi-structured Observation   19

4   Observation as an Experimental Method   29

5   Unstructured Observation: The Rise of
    Ethnography   39

6   Work in Progress   55

7   Visual Ethnography   65

8   Self-Observation   81

9   Ethical Dilemmas   91

10 The Limitations of Observation   99

References   105

Index   109

List of Figures and Tables

Figures

7.1 Ian on his pitch in Glasgow's Argyle Street with
his dog, Misty   72

Tables

1.1 Contrasting structured and unstructured
observation   4
2.1 One-hour recording schedule for street-beggar
study   12
2.2 Frequencies of observed behaviour (those *not*
engaged in active learning) at three-minute
intervals   16
2.3 Individual children 'inactive' at different
observation frequencies   17
3.1 Interview observation checklist   26
7.1 Different qualities of verbal/visual representation 70
7.2 Signifying elements in the photograph of Ian   73

Series Foreword

The success of the first books in this series was encouraging but not entirely surprising. Research is a practical activity and few methods texts, even relatively advanced ones, are sufficiently practical at the level of useable detail. And those hefty, apparently comprehensive, 'introductory' tomes – dispiriting to students – are usually only adequate for writing exam answers: hardly an end in itself.

A further limitation of existing texts is that they tend to present a prescription impossible within the constraints of a modest research project in a real-world setting – or indeed, in anything less than an ideal world. Like any other engagement with reality, research is often a matter of making the best compromise that nonetheless preserves the essential values of a disciplined investigation.

Bill Gillham

Acknowledgements

Clare Cannon word-processed successive drafts of the manuscript – at high speed as the deadline approached – with my wife, Judith, scrutinizing each draft as it appeared. Rowena Gorrie, occupational therapist, provided some material for inclusion in Chapter 3. My colleague Helen McGilp carried out a literature search on the topic of urban street begging relevant to Chapter 6. Chapter 7, dealing with visual ethnography, owes much to the 2007 edition of Sarah Pink's *Doing Visual Ethnography* – strongly recommended in its own right.

A less specific acknowledgement is to my experience, as a psychologist, of having worked in Design Faculties of Art Schools for the past decade, which has expanded my appreciation of the potentiality of observational methods.

1

Why Observe?

Observation has one overpowering claim to validity: it deals not with what people say they do but what they *actually* do – to the extent that their behaviour is open to observation, and insofar as observation is as objective as it seems to be. Two questions follow from this. In the first place why don't we just take what we are told, because surely people know themselves better than anyone else does? And secondly, if observation is more valid why is it not used more often in social research?

For some dimensions of human experience asking people is the only feasible way of finding out, particularly the 'invisible' elements: thoughts, feelings, intentions, attitudes and the like. Sometimes these can be inferred from behaviour but in the main we can only speculate. The question of validity (how accurate these self-reports are) is not a simple one because people 'construct' their understanding of themselves; and how is anyone to say whether these self-constructions are accurate? It is not a meaningful question: such formulations represent how people manage themselves, changing with age and experience, a process of permanent revision in an attempt to find an effective way of being. It is an entirely subjective 'reality' even if sometimes appearing to verge on self-delusion: we all have a preferred way of viewing ourselves.

Words and deeds

Whether people report their *behaviour* accurately is a different matter; and here the notion of accuracy has a different meaning. We can observe what people do and that includes observing ourselves. Comparing observed behaviour with the acknowledged subjectivity of self-perception, it is easy to assign to observation an unchallenged objectivity. Less easy is to acknowledge that observation is to a greater or lesser degree a process of selection and reconstruction. Interestingly, it is research on the validity of witness statements (traditionally highly valued in criminal courts) that has shown how much omission, reconstruction and unvarnished error there can be in such reports.

We can accept that we may not be entirely accurate in our recollection of past events, including our own behaviour. That we may not accurately know how we behave *in the present* is another matter. If you have ever had to keep a work diary as part of a job evaluation exercise you will know that the pattern is often rather different from your unanalysed impression; in particular that the productive elements are fewer than you would like to think. And that is evident at the more mundane level of how we spend our money – an exercise that most of us are driven to at some point when our bank balance is inexplicably depleted or a credit card bill far beyond what was expected.

The simple fact is that we don't normally feel the need to have an explicit record of what we do so that we can't 'know' ourselves in that fashion – and, therefore, cannot be other than approximately accurate. We have an impression of how we conduct ourselves and how other people behave in a range of social situations. In the ordinary business of living that is all we need: self-invigilation is unnecessary. But research requires a more rigorous approach.

In social research on human behaviour survey methods of one kind or another (interviews, questionnaires) predominate. Some are more expensive on time and resources than others; questionnaires are often preferred for that reason. But none is as time-consuming as *observation*; and this is the main answer to our earlier question as to why it is less often used.

Structured observation is the most economical form with its highly specific focus and systematic checking of the elements of behaviour – for example, bullying incidents in a playground; stopping to look at a picture in a gallery; frequency of donations to a street beggar and so on. Here the observation is of the restricted *non-participant* variety. At the other extreme essentially *unstructured participant* observation, typically in the theoretical framework of *ethnography* (usually describing a particular sub-culture in our own society) involves a much longer duration – weeks and usually months, exceptionally even longer than that.

Such groups are investigated in this way for a number of reasons (to be considered later) but also because their members may not be willing, or sufficiently 'organized', to answer questions about themselves. One of the under-recognized weaknesses of survey methods is the implicit assumption that people have their self-knowledge arranged in such a way that they can be easily interrogated about it. This is part of the contemporary expectation in Western society that people should be able to explain themselves. Compliance with such expectations is one reason why self-reports have to be treated with caution: responses to survey questions may be little more than an artefact of the method employed.

Observation and self-report: similarities and differences

Both self-report (as in questionnaires and interviews) and observation techniques can differ in their degree of structure. The first of these may involve short, prescriptive question-and-answer formats that are easily analysed in quantitative terms. Using structured observation schedules which involve the recording and counting of pre-determined categories of behaviour is an almost exact analogy.

On the other hand, interviewing can be largely unstructured, apart from identifying the broad area of interest, following directions determined mainly by those being interviewed. Observation can be similarly open-ended, recording what turns up at a level of fine detail, with analysis deferred (as well as final purposes, research questions, theoretical interpretation etc.).

Whether surveys or various methods of observation are employed, the differing levels of structure lead to different kinds of data being collected. For the researcher the question becomes: what kind of data do I need? Table 1.1 provides a simple contrast.

Table 1.1 Contrasting structured and unstructured observation

Structured	Unstructured
• relatively economical on time (even including the development phase)	• very expensive on time
• data largely quantitative in character	• data largely qualitative
• detached non-participant observation	• participant observation
• data easily summarized	• data require extended presentation
• data essentially superficial	• data capable of analysis of meaning in depth
• limited linkage to social context	• embedded in social context
• not suited to the study of extended and elaborate sequences of behaviour	• behaviour viewed as part of a complex social interaction

This polarized distinction is false in two respects:

- the extremes can be used in combination to complement each other
- the extremes represent points on a graded scale because there are techniques with varying degrees of structure (as is the case with interviews).

A structured observation schedule has to be preceded by an unstructured phase – otherwise how would the researcher know what to focus on? However, this kind of unstructured observation is more likely to be of the detached, non-participant variety (see page 23 for more on this 'fly-on-the-wall' technique).

The need for a combination of structured and unstructured methods commonly arises when the researcher derives an unsatisfactorily impressionistic judgement from participant observation alone. Conversely, it may be that structured, detached data raise more questions than they answer (as in surveys based on questionnaires) so that supplementary participant observation is required to get at what the data actually *mean* (the qualitative dimension).

What do structured and unstructured methods have in common?

The broad common characteristic is that both are *systematic*; because in taking this approach we come to see things, events and the connections between them that would either be overlooked or not recognized as significant. *Detailed recording, in words or images, brings into focus what is there to be seen or understood.*

It is a fallacy to suppose that because something (an object, human behaviour) is within our field of view that we 'see it'. We have all had the experience of 'not seeing' something we were looking for even though it was there to be seen all the time (I commonly 'lose' something on my desk). But there is another and more profound point: we

5

tend not to see things that we do not know about or understand, that we cannot relate to our existing knowledge. Systematic observation: checking, specifying and seeking explanation forces us out of our preconceptions, leading to a shift in understanding.

The uses of observation

The most general use of observation in research is exploratory, as it is in real life. When we take up a new job, enter university, move to a different part of the country (or to a different country), or even just go on holiday to a new region, we look around us. In that novel setting everything is going on presumably as normal; we notice differences, of course, but our main preoccupation is how things work in the social sense, what the 'rules' are: because every social setting operates in a different way. This is a familiar and often surprising experience when we change jobs, even within the same regulated profession, or to another institution governed by the same, standardized legal requirements. A different school, hospital, police force has its own character, operates its own 'rules' within the same regulatory framework. If we have any sense we don't make overt comparisons but 'research' the sub-culture we find ourselves in. This kind of initial, exploratory phase is adaptive: we learn lessons that we can act upon, avoid blundering on in a state of ignorance. It is also widely applicable in the preliminary stage of much social research, from which purpose, questions and methods emerge.

Observation as an *initial* technique may lead to quite different methods in the main study: surveys, problem-focused action research, focused case studies, experiments of one kind or another. None of these would be possible, or sensible, without preliminary observation of an unfamiliar social context. Such early immersion also guides reading and, as

6

the issues are identified, we come to know what to search for in the literature – the beginning of an iterative cycle of first-hand experience and studying the research reports of others.

Observation in multi-method research

In the same way that surveys can give the bigger picture within which more in-depth interviews are nested, so can observation provide a wider descriptive framework. In a school, for example, it would make only limited sense to interview teachers about their views on the official disciplinary policy without some account, by direct observation, of how student behaviour was routinely dealt with. Both approaches have their strengths and limitations; in combination these balance out.

Because of the difficulty of getting a comprehensive picture via any one method in social research, during the past 20 years or so there has been increasing interest in the complementary strengths of different methods. A key text, recommended for further reading (but not for its readability) is Brewer and Hunter's 1989 book *Multi-method Research: A Synthesis of Styles.* Case study research methods (see Gillham, 2000), with the emphasis on multiple sources of evidence, are part of the same movement. The notion of taking multiple perspectives on a complex social phenomenon (teenage pregnancies, for example) is a commonsense one. Interviews, national level statistics and demographic patterns can combine with participant observation – going with these young women on their daily routines, visiting them in their homes, helping them with the practicalities of claiming allowances, and so on – all these factors in combination enable outsiders (perhaps neither young, nor female, nor pregnant, nor poor) to grasp the wider issues. And the observational element adds something vivid and

'real', which may not be apparent even from loosely structured interviews with the teenagers concerned.

How to use this book

We focus here almost exclusively on observation, principally
when used as a main method; other books in the series cover
complementary methods. In total they provide the tools for
real-world social research.

You may have a project in mind – perhaps only at the level
of what interests or intrigues you – but getting into your
research area can be a frustrating business: suitable methods
are your entry gate. However, methods are not just how-to-
do-it; they embody ideas – ways of seeing your topic which
are part of a process of clarification.

In fact it is a myth to suppose that a research project has to
be precisely (or even approximately) specified before you
start. Nor do you have to conduct an extensive preliminary
review of the literature (how would you know what to look
for?). This is not to advocate doing research in a vacuum, in
ignorance of what others have done or thought in your field
of interest. But, in social research in particular, the first step
is practical engagement with your chosen area, with observation (which can differ in character and degree of structure) an ideal technique for gathering some preliminary
data.

2

Structured Observation

For the moment the terms *structured, detached* and *nonparticipant* are used almost interchangeably: that is not quite correct (see page 19) but sufficiently so to equate their meaning. All introductory classifications simplify reality.

Structured observation (specifying *exact* behaviours and recording their frequency over short, usually intermittent, periods of time) is something that figures regularly in textbooks; less often in the real world of research. It has had a vogue in educational research and survivals appear occasionally in Master's dissertations, as I have reason to know. One can understand the appeal of the technique: it renders tangible an approach to complex, fast-moving situations like school classrooms or playgrounds. The fall from favour has much to do with its 'thin' mechanistic quality and, it has to be said, the obsessional complexity of some of the procedures advocated. See, for example, *Flanders' Interaction Analysis Categories* (FIAC) devised by the American educationist of that name (Flanders, 1970) where in classroom observation during a minute, and every three seconds, one of 20 categories of teacher and pupil behaviour is checked. One can only admire the rigour of such a scheme but its use is less than enthralling.

However, the basic principle of identifying people and (precisely) what they do is capable of a more practicable but still valid use. Let us take an example.

Structured observation in practice

I am currently exploring the practice of street begging in Glasgow. This can be approached in several ways: getting anywhere near a full picture is not easy and this is spelt out in Chapter 6 *Work in Progress*.

Begging is commonplace in the city. You may be approached in the street but the focus of my investigation is those who site themselves in a carefully chosen position, usually with a plastic cup for donations. For want of a better term I call these 'stationary' beggars and they are most often encountered in and around the pedestrianized sections of three main shopping streets. To begin with I observed them in an unstructured fashion and for varying periods of time (15–30 minutes) – sufficient for me to see how I might carry out a more structured observation. All the 'stationary' beggars (those who just sit and wait as against those who walk around accosting people in the street) were male; while most of the donations appeared to come from women usually, by my estimate, in the younger age range (under 45).

Event sampling

Event sampling is used when the behaviour of interest is discontinuous and low frequency, where you would miss the events if you didn't observe continuously. The behaviour has to be specified exactly (making a monetary donation, engaging in conversation) so that it can be recorded on an observation schedule in a simple check-mark fashion.

Now, my impression when passing these street beggars was that they didn't get much custom: continuous observation showed a highly variable picture. But it also led me to expand the interaction categories as follows:

- 'silent' donation where nothing is said
- donation plus some conversation
- conversation but no donation.

Men were more likely to come into the first category. The last category, usually male, were different again; I came to describe them as 'hangers on' and some beggars had more of these than others.

In other words, even the simplest scheme requires amplification in practice. The point to watch is that it does not become too fragmented or unmanageable. For example, the 'silent' donation is a bit of a misnomer as I caught a hint of non-verbal communication now and then, usually eye contact, but too subtle for me to be sure of it. Note also that I was trying to identify unambiguous 'chunks of behaviour', not elusive fragments.

Defining the 'events'

What the above discussion demonstrates is that defining a 'simple' event is not all that simple. I had thought initially in terms of a *donation* interaction but, once I had started observing, it became clear that that was not adequate. I had to define the events in terms of the *kind* of interaction. The interactions could have been further divided, for example in terms of different levels of conversation (the odd remark to a longer exchange). I decided against that on grounds of manageability: it is possible to create a recording schedule that is so exhaustive (exhausting?) as to be impractical. What I did was to observe one of the subjects of study for an hour and record each donating 'event'. So I recorded *frequency* (how many times in the hour) and *who* donated (gender and my estimate of age 45+). My first use of the developed schedule produced the results shown in Table 2.1.

Table 2.1 One-hour recording schedule for street beggar study

Date:		*5th February 2007*	**Onset time:**	*12.55 pm*
Subject:		*Ian*	**Location:**	*Argyle Street, Glasgow*
Interaction Categories				
Donors NB age estimates		*Silent donation*	*Donation & conversation*	*Conversation & no donation*
M	45 –	3		
	45 +	2		1
F	45 –	6	2	1
	45 +	3		

The main point is that even when you try to keep it simple you have to develop your categories to be anywhere near adequate; and that there is a preceding phase of development where you try out your initial assumptions following a period of unstructured impressionistic observation. You might think that this preliminary stage should be sufficient to identify the categories. In fact, it is only by attempting to record these events that their limitations become apparent, because you don't really observe in a focused way until you have the task of recording. This being 'work in progress', what is said here is neither a full account nor the last word – see Chapter 6 for a narrative account of this particular project.

Linked events

One of the virtues of continuous structured observation is that you can *link* events over time. It may be something as simple as noting the time someone joins a queue at an enquiry desk up to the time their enquiry is dealt with. Such a start-to-finish observation has multiple uses, for example 'shopping behaviour': a customer browsing a display up to the point of making a purchase. Other examples could be how long a child in a class has to wait to get a response from the teacher; how long people spend scanning an underground map, or reading a product instruction booklet before using the product and so on. This touches on the area of 'experimental observation' (see Chapter 3).

The limits of event sampling

The continuous recording of behavioural events works well when those events are not too frequent: it gets more difficult as the frequency increases, the main strain being on your capacity for sustained attention. This overload experience usually arises when observing several individuals in a group, such as a whole class of children. When the events are very high frequency – happening simultaneously and/or so often that continuous recording verges on the impossible – you have a number of options. These are:

- narrowing your category(ies) so you are observing only one or two types of behaviour *clearly defined*, i.e. picking them out of the flow
- carrying out *time sampling* where you observe, at intervals, for very short periods of time (a few seconds to a few minutes)
- constructing a *narrative* account – essentially unstructured, selective and, to a degree, impressionistic; this takes us out of the 'structured' frame entirely but there comes a point where any kind of specified behavioural sampling is not only impractical but inadequate.

Time sampling

This is also known as *interval sampling* because you observe for a specified duration at specified intervals – like taking a succession of snapshots, an analogy which is pretty close. Sampling means estimating the frequency of events in a continuous time sequence from a much shorter period (or periods) of time. The main practical challenge is deciding on the length of time for the sample estimate; there is a certain amount of trial and error in this.

The general principle is that the higher the frequency of the 'events' the shorter the periods of observation. There is a kind of gradient here: at some point, which can only be determined by the practicalities of recording as well as 'representativeness', the choice moves from *event* sampling to *interval* sampling (or the other way). With discontinuous interval sampling (as in taking a population sample for a survey) the level of representativeness needs to be gauged in some way.

Alternate sampling

Interval sampling has one important advantage in that you can *alternate* the focus of your observation. The focus could be:

- on some individuals in a group, e.g. boys as against girls in a classroom
- on some specific behaviours, e.g. how many children are not 'actively learning' in a classroom setting or more specifically are engaged in a particular learning activity – or not, as the case may be
- on different *sites,* e.g. in a public art gallery how many people are looking at one painting rather than another, or one *kind* of painting rather than another.

The question remains, however: how do you decide on the duration of the 'interval' in practice? Initially you should take a short interval – say every three minutes where you record for perhaps ten seconds – and then work out whether a longer interval (or a shorter duration of observation) would suffice. If the purpose of the research is the difference in gender response to teachers' questions then you might move the focus of recording from boys to girls (and back again) every other recording period or you might cover all the children at the same time. Note that you would have to define in terms of specific behaviours what you mean by a 'response' (volunteering an answer, signalling the desire to do so, following work instructions).

And because children's work in a classroom has a 'developmental' sequence, in that it evolves throughout the lesson, then a consideration for sampling is whether these phases are adequately represented.

'Validating' sampling

In survey research a sample of the population (however defined) is taken because it is much more economical to do so. A 'valid' – i.e. representative – sample is achieved in various ways (not our concern here but see the book in the present series dealing with social surveys (Gillham, 2008)). Validating interval sampling is achieved by taking a given period of observation, dividing it up into, say, three-minute intervals and then calculating whether by taking every other three-minute interval (i.e. every six minutes) you obtain a similar picture to the more frequent sampling. Table 2.2 illustrates a hypothetical example of observed classroom behaviour (children engaged or not in active learning). Here the *intervals* are every three minutes; the period of observation (counting/recording) is ten seconds – but it could be less. It is usually easier to record the 'inactive' children, defined as those who are not:

- reading or writing individually
- choosing a book
- using a computer
- using apparatus or equipment
- involved in making something or painting
- engaged with a teacher or classroom assistant on a learning activity
- working cooperatively with other children.

It is not a difficult matter to record the individual children involved and their gender (you need to be able to identify the children and simply check them at each observation). If you do this ten-second check every three minutes during a 30-minute period you will quickly identify those for whom active learning is a problem; but the total observation time is less than two minutes.

Table 2.2 Frequencies of observed behaviour (those *not* engaged in active learning) at three-minute intervals

	Time line in minutes									
	3	6	9	12	15	18	21	24	27	30
Frequency of observed behaviour	ℍℍ I	IIII	III	IIII	ℍℍ II	ℍℍ	ℍℍ II	ℍℍ III	ℍℍ	ℍℍ I
TOTAL	6	4	3	4	7	5	7	8	5	6

There are two elements here:

- deciding on the length of the interval (when you're *not* recording)
- deciding on the duration of the active recording of behavioural events (a function of the frequency of the behaviour and the time needed for recording).

Duration needs to be only as long as is required to check the behavioural events – a practical question; *frequency* needs to be often enough to give a representative sample. The

16

frequency of observation copes with individual children's on task/off task variation.

Table 2.2 shows that the average number of 'inactive' children at three-minute intervals is 5.5. If we take six-minute intervals it is 5.4: not much in that. But if we are interested in individual children then the higher frequency of observation might be important; for example the hypothetical example in Table 2.3.

Table 2.3 Individual children 'inactive' at different observation frequencies

	Three-minute intervals	Six-minute intervals
Katie	HHH II	III
Billy	HHH	II
Mel	IIII	III
Robert	II	I

In other words the less frequent interval does not differentiate so well in this respect, i.e. those who are more regularly 'inactive' are underestimated.

Why sample?

Since in the above instance you are only 'active' as an observer for less than two minutes out of 30 why not carry out *continuous* monitoring of the children? The answer is that, quite apart from the burden of the task, you don't get as clear a picture. The successive snapshots tell the story with a precision that is not spurious; and you can validate these frequencies against a class-teacher's subjective judgement.

To take another example: if an art student is interested in comparing the public's response to different styles of contemporary painting (e.g. abstract v. representational) in a public art gallery then the task could be to observe how many people stop to look at these different kinds of painting for at least 15 seconds. Looking at paintings is not a momentary business but if no-one stops to look for more than three minutes then a ten-minute interval and 120 seconds for observation would make it unlikely that anyone was counted twice. The student can then move to a room where paintings of the other genre are hung and repeat the exercise; if both kinds are present in the same site then it becomes a simple matter of shifting the observational focus. This is an example of the 'alternate site' situation. Within an hour the number of people looking at each of two paintings is observed every five minutes for 120 seconds, alternating one to the other.

Why not just ask people?

This last example is introduced because it commonly leads to this question: surely people know which kinds of painting they prefer? The answer is that it depends on their knowledge and experience; and their ability to express it. In any case we may give a view or opinion but find our eyes drawn to the kind of abstract painting that we might dismiss in response to a general, hypothetical question. We don't always know what is going to interest or appeal; only our behaviour shows that.

So here we come back to the point made in the first chapter: that you study behaviour not just for its own sake but because it reflects those elusive internal states that underlie what people do, and of which they may not be fully aware.

3

Semi-structured Observation

If observation is a primary technique of real-world social research one can be forgiven for thinking that structured observation, with its 'count' emphasis and fragmented character, is not the best way of doing it. Sometimes that level of specificity is necessary and useful and it is to be hoped that we have done justice to this approach in the preceding chapter.

As a representation of the reality of what people do, structured observation is as accurate as a questionnaire is of what people think. You know exactly what you want to find out and the form of the data is precisely specified. The limitations are roughly the same as for questionnaires: not much scope for discovery and the underlying reasons lag somewhere behind.

However, being relatively unstructured in approach does not mean you don't know what you are looking for. In the semi-structured variety of observation you go in with quite specific questions but they are 'open' so that you cannot predict what you are going to find. It is particularly suited to the kind of research which seeks to identify practical problems people experience; and then what can be done about them.

An example of how this approach works is the study of the difficulties older people experience in maintaining an independent living style. You don't need to be a demographic expert (or a pension fund actuary) to know that we are part of an ageing population, and that old age is accompanied by a range of disabilities, many of them relatively minor. Helping people to manage their disability has a long tradition; the profession of occupational therapy has a distinguished role in this respect. But the problem has become much broader and, in a sense, mainstream.

A major consequence of the ageing process is when people find they cannot cope, or only cope with difficulty, in their normal environment. At a mobility level this is easy to appreciate: stair-lifts, adapted bathrooms and lavatories, wheelchair access, although not cheap, can help older people and their carers with problems that are almost self-evident.

But an accumulation of less conspicuous disabilities can make independent living more difficult and, in total, become as much a barrier as the more high-profile problems. We can go further than that: people often cope well with major disabilities – the conspicuous problems of living. It seems to call forth their emotional resources and a helpful response from others. What wears people down are the multiple, minor defeats of everyday. On their own they may not amount to much: in total they can lead to a non-coping depressive state. At this point we need to take a theoretical side-step.

Ecological psychology

Ecology is a term dinned into us by the media: it's about being 'green' – sensitive to environmental issues. But that is only one application of the term.

Ecological psychology is about the interaction of people and their environment in terms of its effect on their psychological make-up: at the detailed level of the behaviour and mental experience of individuals. It emphasizes that those psychological dimensions are only meaningfully understood *in the context in which they occur*, and that the environment facilitates or constrains people's behavioural or mental state. It is from this standpoint that we can approach the notion of disability. This is not just something about the individual: a disability occurs in a given situation. It is an interactive (person ↔ environment) problem which can be approached from either end or, indeed, from both.

People don't just have to adapt to their environment: their environment can also be adapted to them – at a level of functional detail. A simple example is the problem of lifting and carrying experienced by many people with moderate disabilities. They can be taught more effective, less effortful techniques; as well as being provided with aids that make the tasks easier such as the 'helping hand' – rather like the tool used by litter collectors – that makes it easier to pick things up or pull them towards you, or the *dycem*, a non-slip mat to keep things steady – jars and tins, for example. These are relatively 'minor' problems with simple solutions: they have to be multiplied many times and viewed as part of a persistent daily struggle for many people. Helping them to cope practically is to help them emotionally and a practical focus has to be reckoned in terms of these benefits as well.

Observing the problems of living

You can learn a lot about helping people maintain their independence by talking to them. But this approach is limited for two reasons:

- they may accept their problems as being normal and 'only what you can expect'
- they may not even realize they have difficulties in living for which they could get help, as often people adapt when they don't need to.

21

Inclusive design

An ergonomically-minded designer brings a particular mind-set to issues such as these. Designers are trained to analyse the functional problems posed by the myriad man-made objects that form part of our domestic existence. The purpose of design is not just to produce something that looks good but something that is also reliable *and easy to use.* An important principle is that design which makes life easier for people with disabilities can mean products that are easier to use for everyone. The recent *Focus* range of cars from Ford is an example of this. Designs that only the fully able-bodied can use are *exclusive* – hence the reverse term.

That trend in design exists as a corollary of observational methods that direct the designer's attention. Not that this is just for such specialists: there is a straightforward common-sense dimension to identifying difficulties that points the way to possible solutions.

Take, for example, the case of a man in his seventies who has suffered a stroke that has resulted in a degree of paralysis to the left side of the body. He lives on his own but is still mobile and speech is only slightly impaired. The major problem is the limited use of his left hand – in most people the *sub-dominant* hand. This is not so severe a handicap as it might have been because he was normally right-handed, so it could have been worse. But the problems are numerous, nonetheless, and by no means obvious.

It is instructive to spend an hour or so *as if* your sub-dominant hand were not functional. You can't exactly replicate the difficulties this person might have. But you soon come to see that even a relatively minor disability leads to many problems – some more marked than others. Take something as simple as writing a letter or making a shopping list: you write with your dominant hand but you need the other one to stop the paper from sliding around. This is the kind of thing you don't normally need to think about but the examples are multiple – not just obviously intricate ones like threading a needle but larger movements like holding a cupboard door open with one hand to stop it swinging closed so that you can take something out with the other; and so on.

The context focus

The strategy for observation is straightforward.

An initial period of 'open' observation is required: getting a sense of the person in his or her context, making preliminary notes of particular tasks that look problematic. You ask questions as you go but *watching* is the primary method. Most people can tell you what causes their difficulty but they cannot necessarily analyse it: at least at the level of devising a solution.

It is only by spending time 'on site' and through the routine of a person's day that you can arrive at a 'disability map' highlighting those features which require attention. Occupational therapists in particular are well aware of the problems associated with particular disabilities so that, in many cases, the solutions are readily available. But some are specific to an individual and to a particular context and not so straightforward to resolve.

So, in the case of our hypothetical stroke patient, we may find he is unable to use a conventional cooker because he cannot stoop down and do the two-handed job of taking something out of the oven. A waist-level or microwave oven on a flat surface is one solution. If he likes to heat a tin of soup for his lunch he may have difficulty in using the wall-mounted can-opener – normally holding the tin in the left hand and operating the opener with the right – as the two actions need to be simultaneous. But he can't achieve the necessary left-hand grip on the can. Again this is a case where there are ready-made design solutions – openers with single-handed or even no-hands operation. But there are

23

many other problems not so well-focused – as you will discover from trying out a one-handed style of operation yourself.

Observation in training

In a sense we are all 'disabled' when it comes to operating an unfamiliar and relatively complicated piece of equipment: the controls in a new car, the sequence of operations in a new piece of software or a washing machine with a more elaborate choice of programmes – all of these can have us poring irritably over a not-entirely-clear instructional handbook. Those who produce these manuals know what they're presenting: and that's the problem. They cannot see it from the perspective of the first-time user. It is surprising that more manufacturers don't use the relatively inexpensive medium of a demonstrational DVD. Such things are more easily grasped by observation. That's one point.

The other, and relevant to training, is 'expert' observation of a novice's attempt to use equipment or a technique. Apart from focusing guidance on the actual difficulties of an individual attempting to master the procedure, there are implications for design and instructional guidance.

Training therefore needs to proceed from:

- an informed position based on familiarity with the difficulties likely to be experienced
- an awareness of the importance of *observing* an individual who is learning the procedure.

Teaching and learning

An uncritical assumption these two terms are synonymous: the contrary case is that if there is no learning there has been no teaching. Even the most clear and careful teaching is not enough to guarantee learning; in the same way the present book is not sufficient for the effective practice of the techniques described. The apprentice researcher has to try them out with tutorial guidance and corrective feedback.

The teaching–learning gap is most apparent in the case of practical skills – those which you have to execute. There is a world of difference, for example, in knowing *how* to swim and being *able* to swim. In that case it is fairly obvious.

Demonstration is the critical first stage, where key skills are emphasized and the learner's difficulties anticipated. This is different from observing a smoothly polished performance which lacks an instructional focus; and discourages the novice. The trouble with expert performance is that it looks 'easy' and gives no indication of the training and practice that led up to it – until you try to replicate that low, scooping backhand you observed on the centre court at Wimbledon.

The range of applications is vast: the use of machine tools for engineering apprentices; classroom management skills for probation teachers; dealing with aggressive or unco-operative patients in nursing training; or the handling of people in distress by social workers and others in the 'caring' professions.

Training in research skills is, in many respects, no differ-ent. Research is largely practical, as are its component activities: you need to know how to *do* things – as well as appreciating their intellectual significance. Take, for exam-ple, the use of interview techniques (commonly used in qualitative research). There are methods texts on the sub-ject, some more practical than others; with varying degrees of effort they can be read with a level of (intellectual) understanding. But practical training (which can be self-managed to a large extent) is indispensable. Actually *doing* an interview is, in itself, highly instructive. And this can be built on by making a video recording of your performance and then viewing it perhaps with a supervisor but, in any case, with *structured guidance* as to what to look for. A checklist example to guide observation is given in Table 3.1.

Table 3.1 Interview observation checklist

1. Do you explain the purpose of the interview?
2. Do you introduce yourself clearly – who you are and what research you are involved in?
3. Do you take time to settle in the interviewee, checking if they have any questions they want to ask you?
4. Do you explain how long the interview will take and that you plan to record it (have they agreed to that)?
5. Do the questions you ask, topics you raise, have a developmental sequence where one leads on to the other?
6. Are you sensitive to the direction indicated by the interviewee?
7. Do you allow 'space' for the interviewee to respond?
8. Do you avoid 'portmanteau' questions, i.e. two or more questions joined up?
9. Are your own questions economical in content and style?
10. Do you tend to overtalk or finish off what the interviewee is saying?
11. Do you follow through topics sufficiently?
12. Do you (unobtrusively) 'steer' the interviewee in the direction you want to go?
13. Are you sensitive to the mood and uncertainty of the interviewee?
14. Are you alert to non-verbal signals from the interviewee?
15. Do you make good use of non-verbal communication yourself?
16. Do you round off the interview, e.g. summarizing, checking your understanding of what they have told you?
17. Do you 'close' the interview in an appreciative way?

18. Do you explain what you will be doing with the interview recording?
19. Do you offer to let them know about the outcome of the research?
20. Do you explain how confidentiality is protected?

Note that there are two elements to learning here:

- observation followed by practice
- critical analysis of performance *largely* carried out by the person who is learning (hence the importance of a video recording).

The particular example given here could be paralleled in other domains. It can be applied to the learning of any skilled performance where explicit techniques can be specified; and, as in the instances given, these do not need to be low-level and mechanistic in character. There are levels of skill in any new task, some straightforward and basic (but still important); others more interpretive and evaluative. For instance, thinking in terms of research skills, the use of bibliographic software like *Endnote* involves fundamental how-to-do-it operations that have to be mastered which then lead on to a wide range of applications such as integration with other databases. Becoming confident (and competent) in such procedures should involve following set exercises and then evaluating the results: different dimensions of preparing academic texts – citation, footnotes and endnotes, referencing systems and the like – all part of mastering the use of this important aid to preparing academic texts whether in book, paper or thesis format.

The point needs be laboured no further, except to emphasize that a similar approach (observation, practice, guided *self*-observation) should form part of any learning programme, at all levels and in all areas of skilled performance.

4

Observation as an Experimental Method

We commonly talk of 'experimenting' with things – whether it is a new multi-function mobile phone or an elaborate recipe culled from a magazine – by which we mean trying something out and seeing what happens, what results we get. Formal experiments lie at the heart of scientific research and there are two main kinds: theory testing (*if this theory is correct we ought to get this result*) and significant effects testing (*empirical research*) which is quite close to our commonsense usage above.

Consider, for example, medical researchers evaluating a new drug. A recipe that doesn't work is of little importance; a drug that doesn't do what it is supposed to do can lead to a waste of resources and even damage human health – hence the controlled conditions and elaborate safeguards involved in such research. We shall take lessons from the careful procedures of medical scientists.

Formal experiments

Let us assume that a new drug for treating hypertension (high blood pressure) is being tested.

The scientists would first ask themselves: does the drug have an independent effect on blood pressure (itself a variable phenomenon)? The standard procedure is to use an *experimental* group (who get the drug) and a *control* group (who get an inert placebo). They might also employ multiple experimental groups trying out the drug at different dosage levels.

Obviously they would try out the drug on people who suffer from hypertension, and there are levels of this – mild, moderate and severe. However these human guinea pigs are selected, the medical scientists still have to ensure that the two groups to be compared are equivalent. This is done by allocating patients randomly to each group – note that this is a technical procedure designed to ensure that there is no systematic bias in selecting patients.

The patients are tested before and after the (real or placebo) drug treatment, and here great care has to be taken to ensure:

- no patients know which they have been given
- the doctors administering the 'drug' do not know either
- the medical researchers who measure blood pressure before and after the administration don't know to which group the patients belong.

This kind of *triple-blind study* effectively removes the bias that comes from expectation (by the patients, but also the doctors and researchers). Of course that level or kind of rigour won't be needed in what is to be described here; but it points the lesson that we should be alert to sources of bias in our findings.

A practical example

We live in a world of mass-produced, designed objects. In the previous chapter we stressed the need to observe, naturalistically, the fine detail of daily living, where people have to deal with the, usually minor, challenges of routine practicalities. That can be done systematically but it does not amount to an 'experiment'. In a practical experiment we construct a setting and then observe how different groups (by age or whatever) cope with it: we manipulate or control what we observe.

Designers work to a particular brief and with a particular purpose in mind. A familiar example is that of safety bottle caps – for medicines and potentially toxic household fluids such as bleach, disinfectant and paint stripper. These have been a significant source of harm (sometimes fatal) to young children. Most serious accidents to this age group occur in the home because that is where they spend most of their time. The contribution of design to child safety is an important one, with many successes.

Safety bottle caps, so designed that they require a (presumably) adult level of understanding and dexterity to unscrew them, are a good example. But as with most 'solutions' they can create problems in their turn. A characteristic design is one where you have to squeeze the top at certain points, push down and then turn. This creates difficulties for older adults who have arthritic hands or muscular weakness; but in truth we all have some difficulty with this type of cap. And it can lead to other kinds of accidents – for example to an older person trying to lever the top off.

So we have two problems that require a design solution: bottle caps which can't easily be opened by young children but *can* be opened without difficulty by adults with mild disabilities. How could a design which seeks to overcome these conflicting problems be evaluated?

The experimental setting

We could try out the new design with three groups:

- children aged 3–5 (a particularly vulnerable age)
- bodily able adults aged 25–35 years

31

- adults over 65 with the kind of mild manual disabilities outlined above.

The researcher would give each of them, individually, the 'test' bottle simply saying: *See if you can get this cap off* (in the case of the children first screwing the cap *on* while they watch so that they are 'cued in').

Their attempts would have to be videoed because the designer/researcher would need to analyse each attempt retrospectively. It would also be necessary to *time* each individual because, even if successful, any delay might be critical to safety in young children (as many parents can testify); and conversely might try the patience of older people struggling to remove the cap.

The results of such an experiment can be surprising. For example, we might find that the new design defeats the attempts of all the children, half of the older group with manual disabilities, but also *some* of the physically able younger adult group. That would be interesting in its own right. But the most important element is what lies behind the results and it is here that the video analysis makes its contribution, allowing repeated observation of the same sequence as necessary, showing *how* the individuals attempted to remove the cap and what seemed to be the problem elements.

A short video *interview* could also be used to supplement the observation sequence, asking (the adults) what they found difficult about the operation of the cap.

What we have described comes under the heading of *evaluative research* and it is here that systematic 'experimental' observation is particularly appropriate. Does it work in the way intended? And what lessons can be learned from a study of how the individuals concerned tried to operate the safety cap (or whatever was being tried out)?

Using comparison groups

In the previous, hypothetical, experiment we proposed three *different* age/ability groups, giving them all the same task.

Another approach would be to have groups made up of approximately the same kind of people (loosely matched in terms of age, gender, ability and experience) and give them different versions of the same task, for example evaluating different approaches to software training:

- a group that watched a 'live' demonstration
- a group that studied the manual
- a group that had access to a video demonstration and a 'key points' printed summary.

Note that this is not a tightly controlled conventional experiment seeking significant differences between the groups on some pre- and post-test performance criterion. Rather the different methods would be compared in terms of:

- the kind of questions people asked in training
- the difficulties they experienced in their subsequent use of the software, perhaps against a performance checklist.

We are not out to demonstrate the superiority of Method A over Method B or C; in real life you learn something from observing each method.

So the emphasis may not be quantitative but it is *systematic*. We are after insight into the practicalities of learning a procedure. There will be hints and clues from the successes and difficulties of those using the software; and we can ask them what they found useful or not, as the case may be, in the form of training they were given.

Although the comparisons are carefully specified and the whole procedure systematically organized and analysed, it is a long way from a traditional experiment where you would

have random allocation of subjects to groups, exact equiva-
lence of training times, pre- and post-tests on a precisely
specified performance test (of the *outcome* or *dependent variable*) and so on.

If experimentally-minded social scientists see this as the
thin end of the wedge, they should be warned that our
exposition is about to get wider by taking 'experiments' lit-
erally outside into a real-world setting.

Devising signage systems

A well-designed environmental setting like a road layout or
piece of equipment almost speaks for itself in the sense that
without specific instructions or even too much thought you
know what to do. Ambiguous road layouts or control panels
on a car are at least irritating, at worst can lead to accidents.
Both employ what are known as *signage systems* to supplement the guidance that comes from the overall perception
of the design layout. Such systems almost amount to an
international language and for road signs, in the European
Union at least, are regulated to that end.

Devising signs that are easily and unambiguously read is
an industry in its own right. The most easily read signs (like
primitive languages) are *pictographic*. For example on a video
or DVD player we would all recognize:

$<<<<$ = rewind/return

$>>>>$ = fast forward

Note that the use of multiple arrow heads seems to connote movement; you get something similar in the kind of
road sign that emphasizes you are travelling to the left or
right (or should be!).

On amplifying equipment this kind of visual movement
may be incorporated to show an increase in volume, especially if it has a 'growing' gradient as you press the button.

These pictographic visual clues are fairly straightforward

but there is a range of more abstract signs; and first we need to clarify these different 'written' language systems.

Types of written language

Pictographic signs – where simple schematic picture-signs are employed – are the most basic and straightforward: for example the signs for wheelchair access to lavatories, those for men and women, or baby-changing facilities. Pictographic *languages* are the most primitive because they are the least capable of representing more abstract and complex language functions such as the expression of thought. In western cultures we mostly have an *alphabetic* language system – where the written symbols are linked reasonably directly to the way in which the 'signs' are said.

But the third main type of written language system is *logographic*: that is where the sign represents a *concept*, which may be abstract in character. The *written* Chinese language is logographic – it conveys meaning but not how the signs are *spoken* – thus the two main spoken Chinese languages, Mandarin and Cantonese, are mutually incomprehensible, though the speakers can communicate in writing. This may sound strange but we have a parallel in our own culture in the system of numerals and mathematical symbols; these are almost universal but a Frenchman would probably not understand a Norwegian who 'spoke' a formula such as $3(5^2)/10.54$ – yet both could read it (although to complicate the example most Europeans use a comma to indicate a decimal point). Many established signage systems are 'logographic', i.e. universal in that sense, and they are constantly developing. And product marketing depends heavily on instantly identified logograms – hence *logos* – from the Nike 'swoosh' to the controversial design for the 2012 Olympics.

Testing signage systems

It would be wrong to assume that pictographic signs are always easy and unambiguous to read; also, some of them are 'in between' – for example the skull-and-crossbones sign to indicate danger (why not a graveyard?). Here the picture represents a concept; but there is a limit to how far pictures can depict the abstract. The relationship between sign and symbol, signifier and signified, is too deep a theoretical issue for us to consider here. It is sufficient to say that some 'abstract' symbols are more easily 'read' than others, whether they are conventional or not. Consider what these examples might mean (some more established than others).

$$\Delta \quad = \quad ?$$

$$\square \quad = \quad ?$$

$$\blacksquare\blacksquare \quad = \quad ?$$

$$\male \quad = \quad ?$$

$$\female \quad = \quad ?$$

The last two have a well-established signification of gender – but are you entirely sure which is which? And *why*? (Answers are given at the end of the chapter.)

Signs in context

Signs, like words, are supported in their meaning by the context in which they appear and these contextual factors all have a bearing on whether signs are 'seen' as well as 'read'. You can, of course, test signs as a paper exercise – as above, i.e. what do you think these might mean? But a more adequate test is the *behavioural* response of people to the sign.

This needs to be spelled out because it involves juggling several variables in an actual live setting – too complex and difficult to define for a tightly controlled experiment. Both structured and semi-structured observation have a role here, and perhaps interviewing as well. The *experimental* dimension is the manipulation of the *contextual factors*; we would previously have found out whether people read the signs correctly *once they have seen/noticed them*. So the experiment is about presentational and contextual factors, for example:

- size and colour contrast of signs
- precise location (proximity to what is being signed, 'guidance' from the layout)
- association with/or distinction from other signs (relevant linking, avoiding confusion or ambiguity)
- height at which signs are placed
- 'confusion' factors – the visual busyness of the surroundings.

If signs on equipment are being tested then mock-ups are appropriate but here again other factors come into play (sequence, visibility, size, and so on), all of these being relevant to how, and whether, the signs are read correctly. For example, if on a piece of equipment there is a sequence in operating the controls – whatever signs are used – the signs will be more easily 'read' if they are placed in a left-to-right arrangement in the required order.

In researching these situations video recordings may be useful: the direction of attention, hesitation and uncertainty displayed in relation to public space signage; the number of correct operations of keys etc. on technological equipment. In the latter case the use (and design) of product manuals is an additional dimension. In general it is *unaided* responses that are the primary data. *The more help you need, the less successful the overall design and sign system employed.*

And in all cases, the user dimension is a factor. Different groups – by age, ability, experience – are going to respond differently to 'tasks' of this kind. In the case of specified usage this may not be relevant. But, to repeat a point made earlier: something that works *well* is that which presents fewer problems for everyone.

Answers

Δ, □, ‖ are all taken from a CD player signifying *play, stop* and *pause.*

The gender logograms (M ♂ & F ♀) are taken from the notation used in astronomy for *Mars* and *Venus.*

5

Unstructured Observation: The Rise of Ethnography

Observation can vary in its degree of *structure* – how far the researchers' approach is pre-formed, in the sense of knowing what they want to find out or how they plan to do it. But no research, however open-ended, lacks structure. It would be chaotic if it were. So the chapter heading is not exactly correct.

An alternative is to assign the degree of *participation*, conventionally divided into non-participant and participant varieties. If anything these terms are even more unsatisfactory. No observation is entirely non-participant if there is any contact with, or awareness by, those being observed; but it's relative. Much of what is described as participant observation is not so, in the sense that the researcher is not a normal part of the group being observed, nor does she/he usually behave in a fully participant way in the group's activities (which in some contexts may be minimal). Fully participant observation can only be carried out by an insider: someone who already belongs to the group being researched. Two studies of this kind – by Burgess (1983) of a comprehensive school, and by Holdaway (1983) of a police force – are discussed later. It is sufficient for the moment to keep these limitations in mind.

What is ethnography?

The Oxford English Dictionary gives a first usage of this term as 1842 but it has only come into common use since the 1970s. Before that it was comparatively rare and a classic text of the genre, Whyte's 1943 study of street-corner gangs in Boston, doesn't use the term at all.

So what does it mean? Quite simply ethnography began as the descriptive arm of social anthropology where the focus of the latter was on the study of 'primitive' societies. It aimed to *describe* the rules and practices of a culture. Since the 1970s it has become applied in particular to the study of *sub-cultures* in Western society. Some of these will be reviewed later in detail but it is worth considering briefly the motivation underlying this surge in research activity.

The concept of a 'multi-cultural' society is conventionally applied to a population of different ethnic and religious origins. But an alternative is to view the whole range of essentially distinct minority groups, about whom the majority of outsiders know little, as subjects of sub-cultural study. The range of possibilities is vast: not only anti-social football fans, the chronically unemployed, those in the 'black' economy or casual migrant workers; but also particular communities defined by occupation or affiliation: the informal operation of a hospital, or a prison or a police force; black religious groups, West End gentlemen's clubs, Freemasons; or 'deviant' groups – for example, urban gangs or users of illicit hard drugs. In all cases ethnographers seek to gain an inside perspective, perhaps *covertly* (see Chapter 9); one reason for this research interest being that we are either ignorant of differences or make shorthand, uninformed judgements (adverse or otherwise) about the character of these sub-cultures.

A recurrent theme in such studies is that in taking a defined focus on these minority groups we come to understand mainstream society better. Since, whether viewed as 'deviant' or not, these sub-cultures are often the subject of social or political action, the use or validity of such action is going to depend on an adequate understanding of the group in question.

What do ethnographers do?

The basic procedures are easily summarized.

- They immerse themselves in a particular social setting for an extensive period of time, depending on access to the group. This is usually a matter of months, occasionally more than that: Whyte (1993) spent three years in a 'slum' area of Boston researching for *Street Corner Society*.
- They make protracted observations of what people in that setting do and say.
- They talk to people in the group in a naturalistic way as the occasion arises.
- They may interview *key informants* in the group and iden-tifying these figures is part of the method: someone who will explain to the researcher those elements of social organization which are not easily viewed or self-evident.
- They seek to understand and explicate the rules govern-ing behaviour and social relations in the group and how these relate to the physical and economic context of the setting.
- They keep detailed notes of their observations which they may check out with their key informants.
- They collect any other material which supports the descriptive process or aids understanding – photographs, sketches, videos, or 'documents' of one kind or another.

How is this different from case study research methods?

In terms of the kind of data collected it may not differ at all: both involve accumulating multiple forms of evidence on a

41

social phenomenon of interest, of which no one variety is adequate for explanation on its own.

The difference is in *focus*: ethnography is concerned with elucidating the character of a particular culture. A case study may involve an individual, or individuals, in widely different settings or institutions – such as a national organization of professionals – which is not located in a single or simple setting.

Gaining access

Most ethnographic studies are carried out by people who are outsiders, so for them the key problem is access. How do you gain entry, and acceptance once you're admitted to the group? How do you get into a position where you can achieve understanding? Identifying and establishing trust with key informants is the most important factor.

In Whyte's study the key informant was the gang leader whom he called 'Doc'. A direct quotation conveys the character of this. At their first meeting Doc listened to what he had to say and then responded:

> Well, any nights you want to see anything, I'll take you around. I can take you to the joints – gambling joints – I can take you around to the street corners. Just remember that you're my friend. That's all they need to know. I know these places, and, if I tell them that you're my friend, nobody will bother you. You just tell me what you want to see, and we'll arrange it. (Whyte, 1993, p. 291.)

This extract shows just how fortunate Whyte was, which brings us to an element that does not usually figure in research methods texts: that the social researcher, particularly in the role of ethnographer, is heavily dependent on luck. The converse is that with the best will in the world you can find yourself excluded, treated with suspicion.

In it but not of it

Not all ethnographers are in the position of needing to negotiate access and acceptance. Some ethnographic research is carried out by people who are normal members of the group. Burgess was able to study a Roman Catholic comprehensive school because he was employed as a part-time teacher (but identified and legitimized as a researcher) (Burgess, 1983). Within professional groups that kind of researcher membership, though not without difficulties, is usually a privileged and relatively straightforward business.

With deviant or culturally distinct groups no such fully legitimate membership is possible; so that even if someone gains acceptance that does not imply being seen as 'one of them'. Indeed, any attempt to be 'one of the boys' is likely to be perceived as false. Whyte provides an amusing example of this describing how on one occasion, in the company of the gang, he started swearing 'trying to enter into the spirit of the small talk ... [They] came to a momentary halt as they all stopped and looked at me in surprise. Doc shook his head and said: "Bill, you're not supposed to talk like that. That doesn't sound like you".' Whyte continued: 'I learned that people did not expect me to be just like them; in fact they were interested and pleased to find me different, just so long as I took a friendly interest in them' (*op. cit.*, p. 304).

That last quotation expresses the stance very well and is cited to emphasize that *falsifying* oneself is more likely to create barriers than otherwise. There are exceptions. Patrick's (1973) role in his study of a Glasgow gang was covert (or at least largely so); but he is not typical.

43

The lack of prior theoretical commitment

One of the most striking things about these sub-cultural ethnographic studies is their atheoretical stance. Patrick describes his research as containing 'no new theory, no integrating thesis, no synoptic overview of juvenile or gang delinquency' (Patrick, 1973, p. 155). He cites Merton (1957, p. 93) as calling this type of empirical research 'post factum sociological interpretation' where analysis and explanation take place after the observations have been made and where there is no testing of a pre-designated hypothesis. According to Merton such interpretations 'remain at the level of *plausibility*' (low evidential value).

Ethnographic research by its very nature is not pre-determined even as to broad direction, let alone its theoretical orientation. Whyte (1993) describes how he was 18 months in the field before he knew where his research was going. He also challenged the utility of the conventional prior literature review – a problem he had to grapple with in getting his study accepted for a PhD. In the end he produced a review as a conventional appendix but it bore no organic relation to his work.

Taylor's 1993 literature review in her study of women drug users is conventional (being based on her PhD) but also marks out its irrelevance in the main to the work of an ethnographer studying a very specific group, at least in terms of preparation and orientation.

In Chapter 10 we return to these issues which have major implications for the real-world research process and constitute a challenge to conventional academic thinking.

'Thick description'

If there is a lack of *a priori* theoretical commitment (in advance of the evidence) that does not mean that *interpretation* is not one of the aims of ethnographic research. Clarifying the rules governing social behaviour and the social structure of the 'culture' being studied are primary aims. But the starting point is that of meticulous and detailed description – what the American cultural anthropologist Clifford Geertz calls *thick description*. This term is exemplified in his 1973 book *The Interpretation of Cultures*. Two points he makes are that it is only by detailed description that one will *see* what is there: and that such description is basic to interpretation. Such interpretation can only be supported, as a theoretical argument, if the descriptive style 'takes the reader there'. There may be disagreements about the interpretation but the substantive basis for the theorizing provides a reference point.

In reading ethnographic studies one is struck by the amount of detailed description, typically in a straightforward narrative style, often with extended quotations from individuals in the group being studied; this is characteristic and somehow belies the need for elaborate 'interpretation'. To a large extent the data are allowed to speak for themselves although it has to be noted that a process of *selection* is involved in what is presented. An example of this, taken from Patrick's study of Glasgow gangs, describes the arrival of a district gang leader in a bar.

> A slightly-built boy, no taller than five feet eight, was being pointed out even by some of the barmen. He was dressed in a light-grey suit of the latest fashion, white shirt, and a red tie with a white polka dot and matching handkerchief. His long fair hair was well-groomed, parted just to the left of centre and combed down over his ears. Behind him walked a much taller boy, who looked stronger with broad shoulders and deep chest, wearing a light blue suit and a black casual. In their tour of the bar, Dick [gang leader] led the

45

way, shaking hands with everyone and smiling; Bob (whose name I learned later) followed behind at a respectful distance ... Dick had a few words to say to all members of his gang, refused drink after drink, and accepted the deference of boys and young men much broader and taller than himself. Within twenty minutes they had toured the bar and gone. (Patrick, 1973, p. 44.)

What is immediately evident is that the effort to achieve a clear account of social relations in a specific context results in a good piece of writing. Of course, much descriptive writing in ethnography is much plainer in content: not that this detracts from its significance. Burgess (1983) devotes a section of his book to the informal groupings in the school staff-room with a schematic sketch of where their groups were clustered.

He comments:

I recognized that many of these groups were formed on the basis of the members holding similar positions in the formal organization of the school. None of these groups had an exclusive membership, that is, not all those who sat in the young women's group were either young or female and, likewise, not all those who sat in the heads of houses group were house heads. However, I have given titles to these groups on the basis of their main members and their recognition by other teachers. (Burgess, 1983, p. 73.)

The difficulties of recording

Burgess had the great advantage of overtly (with the knowledge of colleagues) carrying out his research in a setting where making written notes, etc., was a normal activity. When you are engaged in studying gang culture (like Whyte and Patrick) then conspicuous recording may be neither practical nor, indeed (as in Patrick's case) entirely safe. Ditton (1977), in a study of fiddling and petty theft in a bakery, had recourse to making his notes in the only private place available, and on lavatory paper. Whatever the setting, recording what you have seen and heard needs to be carried out as soon as possible. Very shorthand notes can act as prompts; a recommended procedure using these prompts is to expand them soon after in an audio recording, which then becomes another level of data for analysis. However they are made, these notes need to be made close to the time of the events while memory is still clear and vivid.

Street Corner Society: an ethnographic classic

First published in 1943, in Whyte's lifetime this classic text ran to four editions and references here are to the 1993 4th edition. For a book of this kind to be re-issued 50 years after its original publication is some kind of testimony to its enduring worth. Of all the studies cited, it is the one which can be designated as essential reading, even if you read no other.

What Whyte did was to live in a slum area of Boston (the Italian quarter) for three years (1938–40) during which time he married and took his wife there: evidently a man of clear priorities. Coming from an advantaged background himself (with a Junior Fellowship from Harvard) he was concerned to understand the sub-culture, particularly the gang culture, of that area about which there were many judgemental opinions and related explanations, but little real knowledge of what living there and being part of that social network was actually like.

He structured his study of the district from the perspective of the gang and members of it who had their own 'street corner' – in effect a meeting place, hence the title. The focus is on the social structure of what Whyte called 'Cornerville' relating it to the gang culture. So such dimensions as different kinds of 'clubs', social mobility, politics and racketeering are all approached, and interpreted, in this way.

Whyte sought to achieve the insider perspective and comments (Whyte, 1993, p. xvi): 'The middle-class person looks upon the slum district as a formidable mass of confusion, a social chaos. *The insider finds in Cornerville a highly organized and integrated social system* (emphasis added)'. His stance could therefore be described as 'appreciative': but it is an appreciation based on intimate knowledge. The implications of such understanding for social action are discussed in our concluding chapter, and re-appear elsewhere; but one of the main lessons of studying such subcultures is that sound-bite judgements – for example, about drug users – do not stand up to scrutiny.

Here we concentrate on the major contribution Whyte makes to the *process* of carrying out ethnographic research. In the 1993 edition of his book he includes a section dealing with the evolution of *Street Corner Society* (Appendix A, pp. 279–373). Going beyond ethnography it is virtually an exposition of a strategy for real-world research-in-context.

He writes:

> ... I am convinced that the actual evaluation of research ideas does not take place in accord with the formal statements we read on research methods. The ideas grow up in part out of our immersion in the data and out of the whole process of living. Since so much of this process of analysis proceeds on the unconscious level, I am sure that we can never present a full account. (*op. cit.*, p. 280.)

He goes on to describe how his interest in the topic originated and developed: elements typically missing from research reports which conventionally give the explicit 'logical' impression of having emerged from a prior study of the research literature. He describes his initial attempts to prepare outlines of his intended research (a typical requirement for funding purposes) and comments: 'the most impressive thing about them was their remoteness from the actual study I carried out' (p. 285).

The approach he adopted was that of studying the social organization of the community by observing the patterns of interaction between people – what they did and said in their social relations, what rules or *conventions* governed their social behaviour. Because this organization was largely informal: 'Life in Cornerville did not proceed on the basis of formal appointments' (p. 293), he had to spend a lot of time with the group he was studying and from day to day.

The influence of Whyte's study can hardly be overestimated and that is because of the general lessons he provides; it is rare to find a contemporary ethnographic study where it is not included in the bibliography.

A much later criticism of his work which he discusses (pp. 370–2) is that the account is *his* construction of the 'truth'. This *constructivist* perspective is valid to the extent that all knowledge, in the sense of interpretation and explanation *including* the results of scientific experiments, is a matter of choice. Whyte, with characteristic reasonableness, says that it reduces to the argument whether 'my "truth" is better than your "truth" ' (p. 371).

When you have read the book you can form your own judgement.

Urban ethnography: two studies

Here we review two studies carried out in the city of Glasgow, both of which have been cited earlier: Patrick's 1973 account of a juvenile gang and Taylor's 1993 study of female intravenous drug users. Both exemplify the challenges and opportunities awaiting the urban ethnographer. In reading them you come to see the distinctive character of this kind of study: like no other in social research.

The over-powering impression – and it is a seductive one – is of the vivid reality of the material obtained. As one comes to appreciate the commitment involved, in terms of time and coverage, it is easy to understand why such data are scarce; and why society in general so little understands those sub-cultures that exist within it.

Glasgow gangs

Patrick's study is unusual. Working as a young teacher (and looking younger than his age) in what was then known as an 'approved school' he struck up a friendship with one of the older boys, Tim, who invited him to 'come and see for himself' what the gangs were like on the next weekend leave (a usual arrangement at that time); an invitation that with some misgivings he took up.

He describes his investigation as:

> ... a descriptive account of a participant obser-
> vation study of one such gang between October
> 1966 and January 1967. In all I spent just under
> 120 hours in the field; and as my involvement with
> the gang deepened, so the hours lengthened,
> until towards the end of January I was in the
> company of the gang during one weekend from
> seven o'clock on Friday evening until six on
> Sunday morning. (Patrick, 1973, p. 9.)

His research was covert in the sense that he did not identify himself as a researcher but as a friend of Tim's from the approved school who was there for housebreaking. Any doubts as to the ethical stance involved are removed as one reads his account of a culture so violent and dangerous that concealment was the only possible strategy; and not without its risks even then. So, although the amount of fieldwork was limited, it is remarkable that it was obtained at all. Patrick's time in the field was curtailed because of the threat of violence to him (because he'd avoided participation in a weekend gang war).

Not the least of its illuminating qualities is the perspective it offers on the institutions of society; as for example a time when he was taken into custody by the police:

> The police quickly realized that I had no information to give them, and so, finally, they told me to empty my pockets. The moment I put my hands into my trouser pockets to comply with the order, I was punched in the back by one policeman and kicked from behind by another as I fell. After a few more punches and kicks, the police withdrew and the door was locked. (p. 58)

An incidental benefit of this episode was that it validated his acceptance by the gang.

Female drug users

Taylor's study had its own share of dangers, a concern that recurs throughout the book; in fact, no harm came to her, which was a subject of remark.

Her research was more intensive than Patrick's; she recounts how for 15 months she spent most of her days, and many nights, participating in and observing the activities of a group of female injecting drug users in Glasgow. Since she was a married woman with children this shows exceptional

51

dedication arising out of her high level of motivation. She observed 50 such women during this period and with 26 of them carried out in-depth unstructured interviews at the end of the project.

Taylor's stance was 'appreciative' in the sense that she sought not just to observe but to understand the women's behaviour by exploring the meaning they attached to what they did. Without promoting any notion that drug-taking was a 'good thing' she argued that:

> ... against the stereotypical view of pathetic, inadequate individuals, women drug users in this study are shown to be rational, active people making decisions based on the contingencies of their drug-using careers and their roles and status in society. Such an approach also allows the ordinariness as well as the more deviant aspects of their lives to be seen, showing that women drug users have many of the same concerns, fears and hopes as other women. (Taylor, 1993, p. 8.)

Although both studies were radically different in focus there were several common features distinctive to this kind of fieldwork research.

Sponsors and key informants

These are critical to gaining access to the group under study, as previously noted in the case of 'Doc' in *Street Corner Society* (Whyte, 1993) and Tim in Patrick's 1973 study. They are often one and the same. The sponsor validates you and gives you entry: while the key informant answers your questions and generally keeps you briefed and aware. As in Taylor's case this last group may comprise several people. Her sponsor was a local drug worker in the area who was known to, and trusted by, the women. He was able to introduce the first couple of contacts and accompanied her on these occasions. Making more contacts was a slow business at first but gradually, as she became known and accepted (*Are you the woman who is interested in women junkies?*), so the study group expanded. But there was a nucleus of eight women who were her key informants with whom she could raise questions and seek clarification.

'Speaking for themselves'

An obvious criticism of an ethnographer (to be discussed more fully later) is that she/he is interpreting, selecting and so constructing the 'reality' presented. Straight but comprehensive description of events is one strand to counter this (legitimate) objection; reporting spontaneous speech is another. Patrick (1973, p. 16) writes: 'Whenever possible, I shall let events and characters speak for themselves'. Taylor takes an identical stance (1993, p. 7): 'Much of the text allows the women to speak for themselves, describing from their point of view the lifestyles which have evolved round their use of illicit drugs'.

Interestingly, although Taylor and Patrick were born and bred in Glasgow they found the rapid patter in the broad accent of the groups they were studying something of a problem (Taylor, p. 14; Patrick, p. 15) and both found it necessary to ask their informants what particular words meant and to include a glossary in their books.

In the contexts in which both of these researchers were working, on-the-spot note-making was out of the question. Taylor is particularly clear in this respect, but found that by writing up her experiences at the end of each day she could recall detail better than she expected. However, most of the direct quotation came from extended interviews with some of the women at the end of her study.

Risk-taking

As noted above, Patrick had to curtail his investigation because of the threat of physical violence; he certainly witnessed a great deal. He was a witness also in a different sense, that of seeing criminal activity in which he might be seen as complicit.

Taylor (*op. cit.*, p. 20) had a similar concern that 'remained with me throughout the fieldwork [which] arose from the illegal nature of much of the information I came across'. On only one occasion did she find herself in actual physical danger 'from a mentally disturbed drug user who was stabbing people who merely spoke or even looked at him'. She did, however, take precautions, first in her choice of area to work, not giving her home address and making her telephone number ex-directory. But, as she became more confident and 'accepted' she took what might be regarded as risks, on occasion being alone with drug-users, male and female. Real-world research such as this does involve risks because that is what parts of our society are like.

These two studies have been outlined here mainly in terms of their procedure: the roughly generalizable lessons to be gained from them. They are strongly recommended for further reading because the detailed sense of what urban ethnography is like requires this kind of thoughtful reading – summaries and quotations are not enough.

It is first-hand experience that brings these lessons into sharp focus. The next chapter describes some current work of the author on street-begging in Glasgow.

6

Work in Progress

This chapter is written 'as it happened' so that much of it has an episodic quality. The chronological form of presentation also demonstrates the nature of the research process, including the development of the author's thinking.

When I first came to work in Glasgow in the mid-1980s one of the things that struck me was the number of people begging in the street, some apparently more habitual in this respect than others. It is still a common experience to be accosted, sometimes by women or children, to be asked for their 'bus fare home' or some such.

I soon came to see that this casual, direct approach kind of begging was different from those who sited themselves, usually strategically, with a plastic cup in front of them. The latter group, always men, appeared never directly to ask for money. Here there were also two groups: those with a dog and those without. The no-dog group often held a card-board notice in front of them: one, who sited himself next to a cash-point in Buchanan Street, had a card which read: HOMELESS AND HUNGRY – PLEASE HELP – GOD BLESS YOU. Their stance – typically withdrawn, eyes cast down – presented a picture of utter dejection. This may be just a 'style' but whenever I attempted to do so, I was never able to make eye contact, let alone draw them into conversation. I was puzzled as to how I might get to know more about what appeared to be a distinct culture of longstanding.

For some time these street beggars, who seemed to comprise both a shifting and a regular population (I came to recognize faces), were something that remained on the margin of my interest but I was intrigued by the normalcy of this street phenomenon and began to read around the topic (usually only dealt with incidentally). Interestingly, begging never has been illegal in Scotland, as in England where it was made an offence under the 1837 Vagrancy Act. Devine in his book *The Scottish Nation 1700–2000* (1999) describes how begging in Scotland was a recognized, locally-licensed activity (p. 100), in effect part of the pattern of poor relief. Sydney Smith, the early nineteenth-century clerical wit and Canon of St Paul's, writes in a letter dated 4 November 1798 of his impressions on a visit to Scotland:

> I suppose there are at least 3 beggars in this country for every one in England, and there is not here the same just reason for putting an end to the abuse. They beg in a very quiet, gentle way, and thus lose the most productive act of the profession, Importunity. (N. C. Smith [ed.], 1956, p. 12.)

After more than 200 years Sydney Smith's observations still apply in my experience; I disagree, however, with his judgement on the effectiveness of their style (see page 63).

My impression was that those beggars who 'set out their stall' usually with a remarkably docile dog sleeping on a cover, were more 'open' than their more withdrawn brethren. I determined to try and establish contact with one of them and so to get a perspective on this sub-culture which, I suspected, had its own characteristics, unknown except to those voluntary social workers who sought to help the homeless as these men presumably were. However, I didn't want to approach the topic through people with their own preconceptions, however well-informed.

I began by plotting the location of these street beggars in

three, largely pedestrianized, intersecting main shopping streets (Sauchiehall Street, Buchanan Street, Argyle Street) so I came to see how carefully they placed themselves to get a maximum flow of passers-by, balanced against unwanted attention from the police: in that they might be held to be causing an obstruction. It was also apparent that they picked their time of day – across lunch-time being the preferred period.

Making contact

I made a tentative approach to one of the 'regulars' who occupied a pitch on Argyle Street. On the first occasion it was raining and he had had the thoughtful (and witty) notion of erecting a small and colourful women's umbrella over his dog, a brown and white specimen of indeterminate breed. I stopped, commented on this, had a friendly response, put a few coins in his cup, asked him his name (Ian) and told him mine, saying I would drop by again.

Being out of town, it was almost three weeks before I saw Ian next. I dropped some money in his cup, crouched down next to him, said that I was from Strathclyde University doing a study of people like him – and could I ask him questions?

Ian was willing to talk. He told me he was there every day usually from about eleven in the morning to two in the afternoon. I asked if he had a place to 'stay' (i.e. live) and he told me he sometimes stayed with a friend but that he usually slept rough where he could – different places. I asked him whether he had trouble with the police and he talked about this at some length: 'they say I'm in people's way' and that he was sometimes taken into custody. I offered to get him something to eat but he declined. I said that I would drop by again and could I buy him cigarettes? His face lit up at that so I took my chance and asked if I could come back and observe who gave him money. He said he was perfectly happy about that. I arranged to be there the next day.

When I turned up he was clearly waiting for me. He said: 'you've just missed about ten people' I handed over a packet of cigarettes, which he immediately started opening, a box of matches; and a packet of chews for his dog. In characteristically oblique fashion he started talking about his dog (Misty, about nine years old). He was keen to tell me how he'd detected a tumour and took her to the free veterinary service (the PDSA) and the vet couldn't find it but 'I know my dog'. This side-tracked into an account of how he'd tried to leave the dog 'with a lassie' but the dog had looked at him as if to say 'don't do it … '.

As he talked it became clear that he was very attached to Misty ('she sleeps where I sleep') and that having the dog with him on his pitch was not just a ploy to attract custom – although it did, as I was to observe. People often looked at the dog even if they didn't give something.

Ian was a bit uneasy about being observed ('how long is this going to take?') and suggested I sit on a bench about 15 yards away where I would have a good view. Apart from the business of recording I was able to see how Ian regulated his pitch. Periodically he removed larger coins from the plastic cup and put them in a pocket. At only one time did he actually solicit a donation – from a young man part of a group, and as a result of a rapid exchange of Glaswegian banter, incomprehensible to me.

Donations were usually made swiftly and deliberately – in one passing movement, so to speak. As Table 2.1 (page 12) shows, younger women were the most likely to give something and particularly to talk at some length: one young woman crouched down beside him talking and stroking the dog for five minutes. There was only one non-donor who gave Ian and the dog attention. He seemed to be of the type I had noted in my phase of unstructured observations (i.e. 'hangers-on').

I felt that Ian was rather conscious of my observing him but seemed concerned that it should work for me. 'Nae bother', he said when I thanked him.

I tried to get some account of his sources of income; as far as I could understand what he said, begging was his main and most reliable source. My estimate is that he took in at least £15 in that hour but I didn't feel I could ask him directly.

One incidental benefit of an hour's continuous observation was that I gained a sense of the 'street culture': difficult to analyse but with a quite different feel from passing through as a preoccupied shopper. One market researcher, armed with a clipboard like mine, and mistaking my purpose, remarked: 'It's a boring job, isn't it?' I didn't feel I could contradict her . . .

Where next?

From my work so far I could see the following developments:

- determining a focus for a literature search on the culture and practice of begging in Scotland and other urban areas
- building on my relationship with Ian
- attempting to establish similar contact with others like him.

On this last point I soon realized that Ian was unusual in always being at his post: others comprised a relatively shifting population even when the same sites were inhabited. So the question became: what was the 'turnover' and how did these men differ from Ian (if they did)?

I had to be away from Glasgow for almost two months but made a point of looking for Ian the day after my return, supplying myself with a packet of cigarettes.

He had moved his pitch to the other side of the doorway

from his usual place. He greeted me as if I had only been gone a day or two. As I bent down to give him the cigarettes he whispered: 'Do you have any change? I don't usually ask but it's not been a good day', and he nodded towards a police van stationed nearby. I took this as some sort of recognition and gave him what loose change I had, talking to him for a while before I asked him if I could come back to photograph him a couple of days later (illustrated on page 72). 'Nae problem', he said. I had in mind to take a sequence of photographs eventually, but starting off with a single shot to gauge Ian's acceptance of being photo-graphed. I also speculated as to whether video would be a possibility at some later date.

Note that I had decided to focus more on Ian, for the moment, because I felt there was a lot more to learn from studying him and because of the tentative relationship of trust that was being built up. As have others engaged in this kind of urban ethnography, I found myself increasingly interested (concerned?) in Ian's welfare, not just as an object of study.

On the appointed day the weather was fine for photo-graphy and Ian was doing brisk business in the crowded shopping street. I observed that instead of a plastic cup he had a plastic lid with a few (low denomination) coins in it. The effect of this seemed to be that people put the money in his hand. Being more visible it may have been that people felt it too conspicuous to put their contribution in the lid. I didn't ask Ian why he'd made the change, but I doubt that it was deliberate – on a later visit he just had a scrap of plastic bag, weighted down with coins.

I explained that I would be taking about a dozen shots in quick succession, and that I would give him one of the photographs. My impression was that he liked the attention and it occurred to me, really for the first time, that his street pitch was for Ian a part (the main part?) of his social life.

In conversation afterwards he said, quite proudly: 'A lot of people know me. They know I'm always here.' Coming away I felt I was right to allow the pace to go slowly; partly because it seemed wrong to do too much questioning and partly because if you are patient, not only are your half-formed questions often answered but you're likely to be told things it wouldn't occur to you to ask. That was to be borne out at the time of my next visit.

Extending the project

It was only at this stage that I started a search of the journal literature for papers on urban street begging in western countries. This was because I had wanted to see for myself first without preconceptions from the work of others. I would be able to read these sources with a context of my own to which I could relate them.

When I saw Ian about ten days later I said I had a photograph for him and would drop it off the next day. I gave him some change and took the opportunity to ask him how long he had been on his present pitch. After some hesitation he said about eight years and before that he'd been in Sauchiehall Street for two years when he'd had an Alsatian dog. I asked him if he'd had a job before that and he launched into an involved tale, hard to follow, about how he'd been described as a bad influence on 'the others' but I couldn't get it any clearer than that. I have decided that this kind of piecemeal questioning is the only way I can proceed.

Later I went to another regularly inhabited pitch – not always occupied by the same person as far as I could judge – on a pedestrian way between Sauchiehall Street and Bath Street. I found the occupant quite friendly and forthcoming. He said his name was Dougie and that he was there most days between twelve and five 'but sometimes I go out with my girlfriend – I've got kids' and on those occasions a friend 'he sells the *Big Issue*' filled in for him. (More forthcoming than others I've seen on this pitch – perhaps another useful informant here: something to build on.)

Back after about ten days I took Ian one of the photographs I'd taken, which seemed to please him. But he looked troubled so I asked him if he was OK. 'I can't tell you,' he said at first, 'you'll no believe me.' I said that was up to him, but could I help? He shook his head: 'There's a guy over there watching me and when I go he's going to follow me'. I couldn't make out what it was about and Ian refused to identify him. Later that same day I paid a visit to Dougie who seemed disgruntled: 'Nobody's giving me anything'. I dropped a coin in his plastic cup; it was not the moment to ask questions. He remembered me: 'You're Bill aren't you?' So, a small increment.

A week later and Ian greeted me as an old friend. He was eager to show me a photograph of a painting (oil?) of himself and Misty: 'It's a girl from the gallery over the way'. Had he been to the gallery to see it? No, he hadn't. What about the man who'd been watching him at the time of my previous visit: had anything happened? He shook his head: 'He was just a nutcase'. I'd assumed something more sinister; certainly Ian had been very troubled at the time.

I explained that I was only in Glasgow for a few days. Ian grinned: 'You're always away!' – adding sententiously, 'you get a lot of knowledge going to different countries'.

That brief episode confirmed my view that Ian took an interest in people, as people did in him: and that contrary to a superficial impression was not a 'pathetic' character, even if he was financially dependent on others. He was 'good value' in return in a way that Dougie was not.

A month later: a sunny day and Ian had erected an umbrella as a sunshade over Misty. I took the opportunity to ask him if he had any family. He said his mother lived in Glasgow but he hadn't seen her for three years because it was 'nae use', and he had a sister as well but he shook his head. I asked him who would look after him if he were ill.

He said: 'I'm not well now – it's my throat'. He'd mentioned something about that before but I hadn't understood him: to be followed up.

The research literature: a comparative review

In what has been written so far no reference has been made to the research literature on urban street begging and associated factors; indeed none was actually read until a first-hand knowledge base (a restricted one, admittedly) had been established.

Two main studies were identified: one by the housing charity Crisis: *We are Human Too: A Study of People Who Beg* (Murdoch, 1994); and 'Begging, rough sleeping and social exclusion: Implications for social policy' (Kennedy and Fitzpatrick, 2001).

These were relatively large-scale projects. The Crisis report dealt with 145 people who begged in Central London; the paper by Kennedy and Fitzpatrick reported on 66 beggars in Glasgow and Edinburgh. They make fascinating reading and provide more extensive information than in the present chapter. Of interest from the methodological point of view – and relevant to the present book – is that neither is an observational study although Kennedy and Fitzpatrick carried out a brief structured observational audit of who was begging and where.

This lack of observational data leads to a central weakness in the definition of begging: Kennedy and Fitzpatrick (2001, p. 2001) define it as 'asking passers-by for money in a public place'. Now from my observational experience this definition is only true of those who walk around accosting members of the public. Those whom I have called 'stationary' beggars (page 10) do not usually ask for money, even non-verbally by extending a hand. Ian (page 60) seemed to regard this as not what he usually did at all and my observations had also confirmed this. In part, of course, it depends what you mean by 'asking' — having a plastic cup with a few coins in it is a kind of request. But it is necessary to distinguish different *styles* of begging.

In both studies the main method employed was the interview (structured in the case of the Crisis study; described as 'biographical' in the Kennedy and Fitzpatrick study).

The stance taken is that begging is a problem to be dealt with; but Kennedy and Fitzpatrick argue that 'homelessness' is not a sufficient focus and that what is required is 'an individually tailored "resettlement" package which met their particular needs' (*op. cit.*, p. 2012). Both acknowledge that begging is part of a lifestyle: e.g. 'Both rough sleeping and the bed and breakfast/hostel circuit help create a lifestyle that is quite different from that of people with homes and jobs. There was definitely a sense of begging being part of that lifestyle' (Murdoch, 1994, p.10).

Kennedy and Fitzpatrick take the view that 'begging is properly viewed as a product of social exclusion' (p. 2003). But 'social exclusion' is a political notion which presumably places a particular value on 'inclusion'/conformity. In getting to know Ian I have come to understand that his way of life is an adaptive response not just to circumstances but to how and what he feels psychologically comfortable in being. The notion of a 'resettlement' package which met his particular needs is to beg the question: according to whose definition of needs and system of values? This is not an attempt to romanticize his style or situation but to question the assumptions that underlie a mainstream interpretation.

With all that in mind I continue with an observational approach which is more neutral, and seeks to describe and understand the street culture of which beggars are a part. Note that even the limited empirical work I have been able to carry out has enabled me to qualify what I have found in the published research.

7

Visual Ethnography

It seems obvious: if you want to describe a culture, making your account vivid and 'real', what more direct method could there be than the use of visual media? And surely, if photographs and video are used you are dealing with a direct representation of reality rather than one conjured up by words?

The commonsense appeal of this assertion is so strong that it may seem absurd to question or qualify it. In fact, it raises issues both practical and philosophical, not least what is involved in something as apparently 'real' as observation.

How real is visual representation?

We inhabit a world of multimedia visual representation. The ubiquity of television, in particular, is such that for most people it is unthinkable to have a life without it. The constant bombardment of carefully contrived images is an almost inescapable experience. Popular magazines and newspapers are similarly image-dominated, text often having little more than a supplementary role. Being a 'normal' part of our lives they create a cultural unawareness of the fact that we are encountering a mediated reality. But in truth, all 'reality' is mediated by our understanding, however formed.

Of course, at one level we know that television is not 'real', but the distinction is not a sharp one and becomes increasingly blurred with familiarity, to the point that the distinction may no longer be made. But can we ever be unaware that we are dealing with representation? Every morning we see ourselves in the bathroom mirror – except that we don't. What we see is a flat representation of the upper half of the front of our body. We don't see a side or back view, or how we look when moving or in interaction. But, more importantly, because most often forgotten, we see a reverse image: and that is not how we actually are.

Are photographs realistic?

If mirrors are a cultural convention so too are photographs. Wright (1990, p. 6) cited in Pink (2007, p. 33) argues that photographs 'are only perceived as real by cultural convention: they only *appear* realistic because we have been taught to see them as such'.

Even when we accept that in our kind of society photographs reflect a shared convention, they still require to be interpreted; different people won't necessarily put the same construction on the same photograph. This brings us to the heart of the dilemma about visual media: *that all observation is an act of selection and reconstruction.* And what guides that process? We are usually unaware of it.

The fact that we have to interpret a text is easier to appreciate. People get different things from the same book; see it differently, although this is often not intuitively obvious. At the age of 20 I read for the first time Graham Greene's novel *The Heart of the Matter* and, in truth, found it a mystifying experience. Returning to it at the age of 45, I read a different book.

A photograph, or a novel, represents something; but exactly what is to a greater or lesser degree a matter of subjective interpretation and that differs not only from person to person but in the same person over time.

Can photographs lie? We know that photographs of people can be retouched to improve their shape or remove lines and blemishes from the face; while a not infrequent occurrence in political history was to remove discredited or undesirable figures entirely. But more familiar are those newspaper photographs (selected from many) which, in an unfortunate fraction of a second, show politicians looking bewildered or anxious or just plain evasive; trade union leaders with an arm apparently raised in a crypto-fascist salute; members of the royal family appearing bored at official functions. That malign 'construction' of reality has its more innocent counterpart. An ethnographer may take photographs (and select from them) according to barely formulated assumptions. In what sense is that selection 'representative'? Whose 'reality' is it?

Constructing 'reality'

If we accept, as we surely must, that 'realistic' photographs are as much a selective subjective construction as text, that does not mean they are equivalent. They can do different though related things (true of different kinds of visual media: see below).

The sociologist, Sarah Pink, argues for 'a reassessment of the aspects of human experience that images and writing best represent and a related analysis of the relationship between the visual and other senses ... '. (Pink, 2007, p. 3). Different media can do different things; provide different tools for the observer/ethnographer. But before considering that we need to deal with the ubiquity of multimedia representation in relation to experienced reality: a book-length philosophical topic that we have to dispose of in a few paragraphs.

Reality and representation

We know the world only through our representations of it and these are constantly evolving; perhaps only babies have direct, unmediated sensory experience of the world – before they have developed representational abilities – and they will later have no conscious memory of it. These inner representations are mainly in the form of language and mental images, but other sensory representations play their part (movement, touch, taste, smell). Those who are born deaf or blind (or both) develop the latter representational abilities to a remarkable degree: they have no choice.

For most of us verbal language and visual images are the primary modes of representation: we employ developed symbol systems so that these representations can be elaborated. And these are the means by which we know anything, including ourselves. It is probable that we know nothing in a direct, unmediated fashion – even our own self. A pioneer in the development of what has come to be known as *symbolic interactionism* (although it was not a term he used) was G. H. Mead whose major work *Mind, Self and Society* was first published in 1934. His thesis was that in relating to (interacting with) other people we do so *through our symbolic representation of ourselves and those others.*

Observation, and perhaps 'participant' observation in particular, presents the challenge of being alert to the ethnographer's self-representation in relation to the self-construction of the people in the culture being studied. This is the notion of *inter-subjectivity*. So the issue is much more than considering what images and writing best represent, important though that is. These tools of external representation are part of the inter-subjective process.

Now these paragraphs smack of intellectual shadow-play but the issue reduces to the difficulty of knowing another person (the meaning and purpose of what they do; how they perceive themselves and their actions) even within the same culture; even more so when we are interpreting a different culture.

Text and images

This discursive introduction in what is intended to be a practical book is because of the need to draw back from the apparent obviousness of visual 'reality' expressed in the opening paragraphs.

That caution is not intended to devalue visual representation: on the contrary, why not use images to 'describe'? The question is pertinent because most observational studies, even those which deal with an unfamiliar culture or sub-culture, do so almost exclusively in text, an apparently unquestioned practice up to the 1990s.

There are reasons for this omission, apart from an unquestioned convention and the matter of cost – less of an issue now thanks to the digital revolution. These caveats need reflection:

- photography can make 'observation' more intrusive (and more obvious)
- people may object to being photographed
- photography may infringe anonymity
- photography may affect the behaviour of those being observed.

These may be seen as problems of research *procedure* – of the use of photography in the practice of data collection. Putting those issues (partly ethical) to one side for the moment we can turn attention to the different qualities of data in the form of text as against images.

Distinctive characteristics

A simple listing of these in tabular form might be as shown in Table 7.1.

Table 7.1 Different qualities of verbal/visual representation

Text	Images
• can be difficult to visualize what is described	• visualization intrinsic
• 'exploration' structured L → R	• direction of exploration less structured
• less ambiguous	• more ambiguous
• impact progressive	• impact largely immediate
• description and analysis can be integrated	• analytic dimension difficult to express in visual terms

The first and last contrasts here are perhaps those which polarize the media most emphatically.

The old saying that 'a picture is worth a thousand words' is false – they are not equivalent in any ratio. Words may *evoke* but they do not *show*: point one. Point two is that language can be, commonly is, intrinsically more abstract, more analytic, than visual depiction. So the issue is one of recognizing what the different media do best in the research area we are dealing with. As Pink puts it:

> Visual research methods are not purely visual. Rather they pay particular attention to visual aspects of culture. Similarly, they cannot be used independently of other methods; neither a purely visual ethnography nor an exclusively visual approach to culture can exist. (Pink, 2007, p. 21.)

This is not just an argument for what is best expressed in visual terms but also for 'a shift from word-and-sentence-based anthropological thought to image-and-sequence-based anthropological thought' (MacDougall, 1997, p. 292, cited in Pink, *ibid.*, p.11). In other words, a shift in emphasis is required to those visual dimensions of culture that have often been omitted and which constitute a particular form of knowledge. How then is this material to be represented and interpreted?

Images and meaning

Traditionally in the research literature, where they have been used at all, photographs (and film/video) have been treated as 'illustrations' to enhance text. Two elements have been neglected:

1. The 'reading' of photographs – the elements of meaning they convey and how they relate to each other (like words and syntax in text).
2. The extent to which an extended narrative account or 'argument' can be presented in a *sequence* of still photographs: a more comprehensive account (as in extended text) made up of the 'sentences' contained in a single photograph.

Reading photographs

Take as an example the photograph of Ian, the Glasgow street beggar, described in the previous chapter (see p. 72).

Figure 7.1 Ian on his pitch in Glasgow's Argyle Street with his dog, Misty.

At the time of writing this is the only kind of photograph I have taken of him. What are the 'signifiers' – elements that communicate meaning – it contains? Considering this question alerts you to the particular properties of still photographs in observational research.

First, although you get an immediate impression from a photograph, you don't 'see it all at once'. We know this in relatively objective terms from research on visual perception. Using a special camera that records eye movements and fixations, it is clear that the eye inspects a display in a succession of *saccades*: sweeping movements between brief stationary *fixations*. That is, the eye 'reads' the display in a sequential manner. Something very similar, but in a more regulated fashion, occurs in the reading of text. But in both cases the extraction of meaning takes place in the mind of the reader, and it will be constructed to some extent differently from one person to another.

What signifiers can you see in Ian's photograph? And what meanings do you derive from it? Here is my own list of the main elements (Table 7.2).

Table 7.2 Signifying elements in the photograph of Ian

	Signifier	Signified
1	• Ian himself, sitting hunched up, low down, not making eye contact.	• Passivity; deprivation; dependence; social isolation.
2	• The dog Misty sitting on a cover with another cover over her.	• Humanity; a warm relationship; a bond.
3	• The plastic saucer with only a few low denomination coins in it (Ian had previously used a disposable plastic cup).	• No importunity; low expectation; poverty.

4	• Ian's possessions in a plastic bag to one side.	• Impermanence; hand to-mouth existence.

Note that both the identification of signifiers and even more the signified (attributed meaning) is a matter of choice. Nor is there any implication that Ian has consciously thought through, in any analytic fashion, the elements of his appeal. But, to take point (1): had Ian been sitting on a chair, or even a cushion, the appeal would have been lessened; as it is he is sitting on the cold, hard pavement. Point (2) there is (to me) no suggestion of artifice in the presence of Ian's dog, even though it is commonplace for street beggars; but without it the appeal would certainly be less. Point (3): the throw-away plastic saucer (or cup) itself has layers of meaning; consider the difference a collecting box would make (and the meanings that would connote). And point (4) a neat rucksack (or even a very shabby one) would connote different qualities/meanings from the disposable plastic bag.

Now all of these interpretations are *my* constructions: *meaning is always an attribute.* There might well be agreement, perhaps negotiated, between different people. But to return in this practical example to themes discussed earlier, although there is a physically 'objective' photograph, interpretations of it are necessarily subjective. These 'interpretations' are part of research data, and differing judgements can be compared *including one's own changed judgements over time.* I see Ian differently now from my first impression of someone passive and pathetic. Note that this whole issue is quite different from the positivist psychometric notion of *reliability* (a technical term relating to the consistency of observations or test scores) and which implies that there is a true reality and that observers/interpreters are flawed instruments in the recording of it.

Every picture tells a story

But it has to be *read* – as demonstrated above. A photograph with its signified elements is not like a list of isolated words: these elements are part of a (visually) structured relationship. We have used words to demonstrate it in this instance, but what is required is a more analytic approach to reading images; to repeat the point, you don't just 'see' them. The need is to establish (non-constraining) conventions for reading visual observational material so that the contribution of these kinds of data is given fuller recognition.

The challenge for the researcher is well expressed by Pink (2007, p. 6) when she writes:

> This means abandoning the possibility of a purely objective social science and rejecting the idea that the written word is essentially a superior medium of ethnographic representation. While images should not necessarily replace words as the dominant mode of research or representation, *they should be regarded as an equally meaningful element of ethnographic work* (emphasis added).

But this kind of call to action is no more than rhetoric unless it can be translated into the detail of practice.

Photographic sequences as a structured narrative

Chapter 2 described how I first observed and recorded interaction between members of the public and Ian in Glasgow's Argyle Street. As I did so I could see that his experience as a street beggar could be told as a sequence of wordless photographic images which could be 'read' as a textual narrative could be read. What is suggested here is that the practice of visual ethnography should employ the universal notion and use of narrative as (to borrow a term from linguistics) a kind of *frame grammar* – a unit of meaning between a paragraph and a complete account.

One might call these 'anecdotes', but note that this typically has pejorative connotations (*it's merely anecdotal evidence*, etc.). Yet anecdotal narratives are how people understand themselves, how they *construct* themselves. The American psychologist Jerome Bruner, in an important paper entitled 'Life as narrative' (1987), gives to narrative the primary role in self-construction.

> I believe that the ways of telling and the ways of conceptualizing that go with narrative forms become so habitual that they finally become recipes for structuring experience itself, for laying down routes into memory, for not only guiding the life narrative up to the present but directing it into the future. I have argued that a life as led is inseparable from a life as told – or more bluntly, a life is not 'how it was' but how it is interpreted and reinterpreted, told and retold. (Bruner, 1987, p. 31.)

For researchers adhering to the scientific-realist tradition this can be difficult to take. What about *objective* validity?

The dilemma (for such adherents at least) is apparent when considering interview data. In the kind of interviews which are relatively unstructured: that is, where the structure and content are largely determined by the interviewee, then the 'validity' of the interview is a function of the freedom interviewees have to tell their story. A common objection to this is that people are 'just telling stories' and 'how would you know they were true?' To which the answer is: how else would they do it? And: what would a 'true' account be like?

Selecting elements for a narrative

Any photography or video used by an ethnographic researcher to present a narrative account of the culture being studied is the researcher's own composition: some material is selected for inclusion and other material is left out.

In that sense it is a partial and also an optional account. It is not wrong to do so, provided that there is an explicit awareness that such a process is open to challenge, together with a justification for the selection process. This process of *content analysis* has a parallel in writing an account of an interview where substantive statements are selected and categorized and then interpreted, and where the researcher has to show the successive stages of data selection and reduction.

The use of video

Video might seem to get round the issue of the process of selection which is self-evident in still photographs. Certainly continuous filming of a sequence of events does demon-strate the chronological relationship as well as providing more options for the abstraction of specific elements. But what is put in front of the camera is still a matter for choice; and editing down carries that process further – hence the common complaint of politicians that they have been quo-ted or shown 'out of context', perhaps with some justice. But there it is a matter of journalistic priorities where the imperative is to 'get a story' which grabs attention rather than the plainer and more balanced priority of a researcher to present a valid and representative account.

The almost continuous character of video recording does leave many interpretive options open. Of these perhaps the repeated re-running of sequences is the most important, making it possible to see elusive aspects, especially of social interactions, which one might miss on a single take. In the days when video was an exciting new toy for researchers, expensive and cumbersome as it was, I was working in a university department of psychology where there was much interest in the early stages of interactive communication between mothers and their babies. So fleeting were some aspects of this interaction, that it was only apparent from the repeated viewing and analysis of the same video sequences.

In ethnography something similar is possible, not least the more detailed reading of narrative sequences from the same stretch of recording. I am particularly aware of the value this would have in the street beggar study, especially in the area of 'donor' behaviour.

Ethnographic collaboration with members of the 'culture' being studied

Human research, even of the culturally sensitive variety, can be seen as something done to people, the passive recipients of the researcher's attention. But perhaps this is to overstate the case. The appeal of ethnographic research is a lot to do with the personal relationships – sometimes enduring long past the period of formal study – that are established between the researcher and those in the community; to the extent that a kind of research partnership is established.

Whyte (1993, p. 31), describing his relationship with Doc, the gang leader, writes:

> As we spent more time together, I ceased to treat him as a passive informant. I discussed with him quite frankly what I was trying to do, what problems were puzzling me, and so on. Much of our time was spent in this discussion of ideas and

observations, so that Doc became, in a very real sense, a collaborator in the research.

This is, of course, a wider issue than a consideration of the selection and interpretation of visual material, wider than ethnography. In any social research checking things out with members of the group being studied at least qualifies the researchers' interpretations and may reconstruct them entirely. The frame of knowledge of those in the community, not least their knowledge of the 'historical' background of current events, means they bring to the current situation perspectives that are not apparent from observation. When we are considering the interpretation of photographs and video, the meaning(s) of what is represented may only be fully appreciated with this kind of help; and there may be different views on this within the community.

There is a difference between checking out one's understanding of visual data, and seeking the collaboration of those in the 'culture' in collecting such material: for example, asking them to take photographs using disposable cameras of the patterns and practices of research interest, or asking to see photographs they have taken themselves for other reasons. The events that people choose to record are part of the meaning they attribute to the world they live in. This kind of material may not have been made or retained for research purposes but can still form part of what an ethnographer collects, if it fits the broad frame of the investigation.

8

Self-Observation

Self-observation is best known as a way of enhancing performance, via video recording, widely used in interview training. Actors whose performances are filmed have long had the advantage over the rest of us of knowing how they look and behave. That kind of feedback can have a salutary effect, not always conscious. But here we are concerned with self-observation *as a research method*, and one which deals not just, or even mainly, with 'external' behaviour.

Research and objectivity

Research is commonly viewed as involving the objective appraisal of 'evidence' which can be independently checked and, where possible, measured. How can subjective experience ever meet that criterion? It doesn't and if that *is* the criterion for the admissibility of research evidence then all our mental experience goes out of the window. In research terms self-observation is a distinct methodology (way of knowing) and the appropriate approach for some areas of human knowledge; if not the only possible one.

We still have to consider why it should be so widely held that research is an 'objective' process. While some philosophers of science, notably Karl Popper in *The Logic of Scientific Discovery* (1959), have expounded precisely this case, the main influence on popular understanding is likely to stem from the way research findings are usually presented in the media, without qualification, as proven fact. And this in turn derives from the way academic papers are constructed and the style of presentation employed. These are conventionally written in an 'objective' depersonalized style: where the use of first person pronouns (I, we, etc.) is largely excluded (an editor once said to me that it detracted from the authority of the writing). By the same token the passive voice is preferred to the active ('it was found' rather than 'we found'); and so on. Yet the papers are written by individuals, with their own motives, purposes and preferences.

Research as 'adventures of the mind'

Some kinds of research are inextricably individual. In scientific research it is those early stages of investigation which Medawar (1964) called 'adventures of the mind'. It is during these stages that the foundations of what will later be constructed more formally are laid down. In a sense this is where the real conceptual discoveries are made though rarely reported in that way, being later reconstructed into the formal logic of a scientific paper.

In the arts the process of research is almost entirely made up of these 'adventures' experienced as a part of practice, but they may also go unreported because the artist is concentrating on the practical or conceptual resolution of the creative problem. Particularly in the visual arts there is a resistance to taking a self-observing research stance: a fear that it will interfere with a delicate process, distract the artist from the main purpose, damaging or even destroying the creative spark. Almost certainly a mistaken view it is, nonetheless, one that has been firmly held.

That such a process of self-observation might actually add to self-knowledge and facilitate artistic development is only slowly gaining ground (see Gillham and McGilp, 2007). As well as enhancing practice it also offers the potential to develop a new research methodology, as relevant to the social and natural sciences as it is to the 'subjective' world of the arts. Certainly in the social sciences the scientific-realist position, so long predominant, is in retreat before an increasing awareness that objective realism is a doubtful commodity when applied not just to people's (mental) constructions of themselves and their social world, but also to how researchers view social behaviour.

This all sounds very well but needs to be translated into practical detail. We shall argue here that self-observation gives access to material – particularly mental events – that could hardly be obtained in any other way.

Research as a creative process

Thoughts, feelings, insights, intentions and discoveries in understanding are all things that are more or less invisible. And usually they go unrecorded, the exceptions typically being fragmentary – and so interesting that one can only regret that more of this material has not been preserved. Ghiselin's (1985) book dealing with the creative process is made up of fragments of writing by leading creative figures of the past 250 years from across the arts and sciences, which provide a fascinating insight into their ways of working. Of particular note are the commonalities across radically different disciplines: for example the role of the unconscious in mathematical creation (Poincaré) and poetry (Amy Lowell).

Creativity is much discussed in a facile, abstract fashion which leaves us none the wiser. Here we define it as what characterizes the way that original work of quality is produced: in other words, what is distinctive about people whom we would describe as truly creative? Everyone seems to agree that creativity is to be valued without, at a level of detail, appreciating the conditions, both internal and external, that foster it.

Self-observation provides a way into this level of detailed recording which, as we noted above, has no parallel method. The observer is always present in us; and as with other methods the challenge is to make the process of observation more systematic and analytic in approach.

Recording the process

In the busy work of pursuing a particular outcome (whatever it happens to be) the details of *process* – which may be as important as the result – are often discarded and obscured, irretrievably lost.

But there is more to recording the process than the preservation of material that may later be viewed as important. Agnew (1993), a design historian writing about the unrecorded history of the development of the Spitfire in the 1930s and 1940s, argues for 'a new kind of comprehensiveness in the most creative stages of design ... The insight ... is often more general in its implications than the ... solution that follows it. All too often the insight may later be entirely lost' (p. 129).

The act of recording means that those who 'create' come to understand better how they work so that they can enhance their performance – rather than 'interfering' with it.

What should be recorded?

This material can be divided loosely into internal and external evidence. We shall deal with the latter first. External evidence could of course be 'observed' by others, if they

84

were always present. So, it's anything that can be seen or heard, for example:

- notes, sketches
- letters, reports
- plans, models, prototypes
- photographs, video recordings
- successive revisions (thoughts written down)
- audio recordings (thoughts spoken)
- material by others which has been used in some way
- diary, journal, log-book.

What is apparent here is first, that a deliberate policy of preserving those elements is involved and second, that they have to be stored in a way which renders them accessible – a particular consideration because there may be a lot of material. Crucially there has also to be a conscious habit of keeping a record of those mental events or habits of behaviour which otherwise would not be externalized at all – evident from some of the items listed above.

Perhaps the most important of these is the log-book (sometimes referred to as a diary or journal) in which are recorded those elements which otherwise fade very quickly, for example:

- origins of ideas (things read or talked about, observed or experienced)
- initial purposes/directions
- hunches, insights, intuitions, i.e. the kinds of thing that are hard to make explicit
- difficulties, uncertainties, problems (and their resolution)
- discoveries, especially reformulations
- refining of ideas and methods
  – and so on.

Deciding what to record has to err on the generous side; not least because what can appear a minor element at the time (a passing doubt, a simple notion) might turn out to presage more significant consequences.

In many ways it is this recording of 'in-the-head' material that is the more important part of the methodology. And it is often only fully appreciated and understood when reviewed *as it occurred* and in chronological order. This last has its own kind of logic in that the relationship between elements needs to be understood in terms of their sequence in the time-frame, which may not be 'logical' in other terms. The great virtue is the recording of the research process *as it happens* and you get no real awareness of this from reading conventional academic reports. The structure of these is often misleading if one seeks to understand how the research evolved. There are here two levels of *discourse*: the formal reconstructed logic of an academic paper and what might be described as the 'chronologic' of a narrative account. Neither is intrinsically right or wrong, they serve different purposes; but the narrative format constitutes a truer account of the *process*.

Observing how we work

The physical, habitual and social context of how we work or research is part of the picture. We don't just exist in terms of what goes on inside our head.

Of these the least recognized (but not the least impor-tant) are those habits of work – perhaps routine – which support the research/creative activity. In scientific papers we may find details of the investigatory *procedures* employed but not those more mundane aspects of practice within which they are nested. Sometimes these routines surface inciden-tally in autobiographical writing or interviews. Thomas Mann (cited in John-Steiner, 1997) wrote just a page-and-a-half of his novels each day; and it took him the whole morning to do so. The immensely successful Victorian novelist, Anthony Trollope, gave a candid description of his working habits in his autobiography, describing how he 'dragged inspiration in by the heels at half-past-nine every morning', a disclosure which shocked his readership and caused the sale of his books to decline.

Writers have been the most likely to describe their work patterns. Victor Hugo wrote standing at a desk. Conan Doyle often wrote his stories at a small table in the family drawing room amidst the buzz of conversation. Others, such as Somerset Maugham, could only work in strict isolation; in his case choosing to write in a hut at the bottom of the garden. And Ernest Hemingway never talked about a book he was working on because he knew that would cause it to abort.

A series of anecdotes: but to the point. Take a moment to consider how *you* work. What are your habits and routines? What setting facilitates the process? What things have an adverse affect? When do you do your most productive work? How far do you plan what you are doing in advance?

Again you have to think like an observer who is always present; and can read your mind.

Reviewing the raw material from self-observation

A self-observation research procedure generates a lot of material. Its collection needs to be organized from the start, and progressively edited down. A good habit to develop is to write a regular *review summary* (at least monthly and perhaps more often than that – it depends on the pace of the activity). These then become part of your documented process. What goes into this record?

Research reports, even of a conventional kind, now commonly include visual material of high quality. True, this is mainly illustrative in character but as technology has improved, particularly the easy weaving in of sequences of images and text, so has an appreciation of the parity between the verbal and the visual. The latter has traditionally been assigned a subordinate status. But, in research narrative terms, images can make a parallel argument or case in a way unique to that medium.

If the substantive content of the creative research process is visual (for example in areas as diverse as technological product development or fashion design) then it may be text that is the subordinate element. This is not an attempted inversion of traditional practice, nor does it underrate the distinctive qualities of text. Language has the special quality (like mathematics) of dealing with the abstract and 'invisible'. There is a limit to how far visual material can be analysed, interpreted or evaluated in purely visual terms.

Producing an edited account

We'll stay with the notion of a narrative made up of verbal and visual elements because this requires the more innovative modes of presentation. The manipulation of text and images using software which, with minimal training and practice, is within the competence of anyone who is computer-literate is one of the major contributions of IT to the recording and presentation of research. It is, in truth, so seductively easy that such reports can give a favourable impression which may not be borne out by a critical review of their content.

Probably the most versatile graphic design software is *InDesign*, which has many advanced features, but is capable of a basic use with very satisfactory results. It does, however, require training by someone who *is* expert and who can set the boundaries within which the amateur will not get lost. *PowerPoint* is also capable of producing a flexible narrative and, because people are usually more familiar with it, in general offers an easier approach.

Producing an edited narrative which does justice to the

research process, and yet doesn't lose the reader, is not something a computer can do for you. This is where the human brain is irreplaceable. The French writer and aviator Antoine de Saint-Exupéry said: 'A book is not finished when you have nothing more to add, but when you have nothing more to take away'. In other words, deletions and simplifications are a major part of the process.

What use is such an account to anyone else?

We are (most of us) very interested in ourselves and routinely engage in self-scrutiny at one level or another. But we do not usually seek to impose that activity on other people. Treating oneself as an object of formal research is another matter. The purpose of research is to make some contribution to knowledge: what can self-observational research offer?

Self-indulgent speculation of the 'who-am-I-and-why-am-I-here' variety, sometimes passed off as 'reflective learning', has little to offer; nor do grandiose quasi-philosophical speculations. It is essentially a down-to-earth business but one where the 'insider' perspective is critical to understanding: where thoughts, feelings, perceptions – as well as what you do or make or what happens to you – are a necessary part of a complete picture.

In this chapter we have focused on self-observation as a way of studying the creative process. But that experiential approach has much to offer in other aspects of the human condition. For example:

- the onset, course, treatment and recovery from mental illness
- the process of retirement or of being made redundant in mid-life
- taking a degree as a mature student

- setting up your own business.

There is a good deal of formal 'objective' evidence, often statistical in character, about all of these; but such sources add little to our understanding of the actual experience. Conversely, insight gained through experiential accounts may radically alter our interpretation of these kinds of formal data.

9

Ethical Dilemmas

How would you feel about being observed systematically, whether for research or any other purpose? There is an intuitive, hard-to-define sense of unease in that awareness which probably has its psychological roots in the feeling that being under surveillance is controlling and, in that way, dehumanizing. George Orwell employed this dimension of veiled threat in his novel *Nineteen Eighty-Four* (Big Brother is watching you); Alfred Hitchcock was a master of the ambiguity of observation in his films (the impassive policeman with opaque sunglasses in *Psycho*). And the French philosopher (if that is what he was) Michel Foucault saw in observation the fine grain of an impersonal social power of control, most clearly manifested today by the widespread use of closed-circuit television – interestingly, like most forms of indiscriminate control, justified as in the public good.

There is then an uneasy position for the researcher who adopts observation techniques. By what right do you use them; and what is the effect on the human relationship (observer↔observed) of so doing? So far we have gone ahead with the practical exposition of methods with only an occasional glance at the ethical dilemmas they pose. We now need to consider these in more detail.

The regulation and control of personal data

The past 20 years have seen an increase in awareness – among the wider community, as well as those engaged in 'people' research – of the ethical concerns surrounding what is done *to* people and how information about them is collated, stored and *used*. The area of personal information was dealt with in the UK at a legislative level in the 1984 Data Protection Act, further qualified by directives from the European Union. However, its implications have been slow to penetrate the detail of practice. It is a progressive piece of legislation in the sense that its powers are regularly updated and extended.

That's a formal framework; at the informal level people have become more conscious of, and sensitive to, the issues surrounding personal information – however obtained. Requests by researchers and others can be seen as intrusive. 'Observation' in this context becomes another kind of intrusion, with a quality all of its own.

The issue of consent

Informed consent is now a standard requirement by universities and other regulatory bodies when human subjects are involved directly, i.e. by their active participation or through demands being made of them.

The passive participation involved in most observation techniques may seem to be in a different case, particularly if what is being observed is 'public' behaviour. What you do in public can hardly be claimed to be private, so here, perhaps, observation should not be claimed as an intrusion into privacy. Put that way it gives pause for thought. Do we do not have a sense of privacy in public? Is, for example, being photographed against your will (like those high in media attention) not intrusive? And what is the photograph being taken *for*? If it is going to be published/distributed/ reproduced, isn't an additional level of consent involved?

Ian, the Glasgow street beggar whose photograph appears on page 72, gave me his consent a few days in advance of the actual photograph being taken: I didn't just turn up with a camera. In the same way I asked his prior agreement to carrying out a systematic period of observation. I also told him that I might want to include the photograph in a book.

In case this sounds too smug let me qualify it by saying that, to some extent, I was capitalizing on our friendly relationship: I gave him money (and cigarettes, which did feel like a bribe); something a bit uneasy there. But he knew what I was doing even if he didn't fully understand it. If people don't know they are being observed, or are the objects of research, does this not border on deception? And is that ever justified?

Covert and overt observation

We need to make a twofold distinction here:

- *covert* observation (where people don't know they're being 'observed' in the research sense) and *overt* observation, where they are being observed with their knowledge or in a self-evident fashion
- observation in an *open setting,* i.e. a public place – in the street or a department store or on the beach, for example; and in a *closed* setting which is not open to the public in any comprehensive sense – the professional side of a hospital, a school, a police station.

So there is a 2x2 classification here, e.g. overt/covert and open/closed. Covert observation in a closed setting is the most ethically contentious of all, and is commonly used in what, for want of a better term, is called 'investigative journalism'. As I write there is a news item about a journalist who obtained employment in a privately-run prison with startling results. Whatever the accuracy or general validity of the findings in this kind of investigation, the (presumed) ethical justification is that these are serious matters which would not have come to light in any other way.

Is such an approach justified in formal research when the concern is to construct a valid and balanced picture rather than to focus on sensational misdoings? A case in point is the study of a police force by Holdaway (1983). We are not proposing to recount this study but rather to focus on the ethical dilemmas it posed for him (as a police sergeant with supervisory responsibilities).

Holdaway's study

The author of the study, published in book form, was in the unique position of being a serving police officer, with the rank and responsibilities of sergeant as well as a sociologist; and, incidentally, an ordained worker priest in the Anglican Church.

Not surprisingly Holdaway gives extensive consideration to the ethical issues surrounding his investigation:

> ... the case for covert research is strengthened by the central and powerful situation of the police within our social structure ... [The present study] is justified by my assessment of the power of the police within British society and the secretive character of the force. This does not mean that covert research into powerful groups is ethical while that into less powerful ones is not ... neither is it to advocate a sensational type of sociology in which rigorous analysis of evidence gives way to moral crusading. (Holdaway, 1983, p. 5.)

So his stance is very far from that of the sensation-seeking of journalists whose aim appears to be to expose and humiliate; whatever the rights or wrongs of what they report, it is certainly not appreciative in the sense of being even-handed. Holdaway reports going with colleagues to see a young mother whose baby had died suddenly, describing their reactions: 'incidents like this reminded me of the demanding work required of the police, and of their humanity ... ' (*op. cit.,* p. 7).

What comes out of his study is an appreciation of the ethical problems for front-line police officers who have to enact legislative requirements and the high profile policies of the senior ranks. One senior officer said to him: 'policemen must be willing to cut corners or else they would never get their job done' (p. 8); and he cites an American study (Westley, 1970, p. 17) which argues that:

> ... even if the law were refined and clarified to ease the burden of enforcement ... the intentions of legislation or of any police instrument would be retained in the process of their translation from the written word to police antics on the street ... police organization is directed not by legal and administrative rules to which police actions approximate but by a series of interpretations by lower ranks which vie with legalistic and other rules.

Within Holdaway's study there are accounts of illegal police behaviour (physical abuse of suspects, mainly witnessed only by other lower-ranking officers) but he attempts to maintain a morally even-handed perspective; that is, achieving an understanding of what serving police officers have to do to manage the demands and stresses of the job.

Witnessing illegal/criminal behaviour

There is a conflict here, not confined to covert research. Any ethnographic study of 'deviant' groups within our society is going to put the researcher in the morally ambiguous position of being a witness to criminal behaviour. Taylor (1993) gives a number of examples of this and her dilemma in doing so: witnessing the sale and distribution of illicit drugs, shop-lifting by some of the women drug-users, once in her company. What does the researcher do in such a situation? Because the conflict of responsibility is real.

Observational research presents moral dilemmas which are far removed from an antiseptic observance of the 'ethical rules' governing research practice; and they are apparent, with a little reflection, at every turn.

'Ownership' of the observations

If people are aware they are being observed, and have 'consented' to it in one way or another, does that dispose of the ethical issues? In two key respects it does not.

In a research interview there are several layers of consent and, of course, the person being interviewed largely determines what they have to say, i.e. there is a degree of *control* on their part. More than that, it is good practice (not just from an ethical standpoint) to give interviewees the chance to check a transcript so that they know what they've said, at that level, and have the opportunity to check or correct it. In a sense they come to 'own' it.

Observation in written form does not have that same quality of ownership. More than that, and without indulging in the intellectual rhetoric of constructivism, it is the *observer's* account – and interpretation – of what has been observed. This issue was discussed in Chapter 7 and we do not need to go over the ground again, but it does indicate the practical and ethical need to check out the observational account with at least one member of the group involved.

An ethnographic report is 'constructed' in two ways:

- what is selected (and conversely what is excluded) in the report
- the significance or meaning attached to what is reported.

At a commonsense level and when expressed like that, the need for those under scrutiny to know and perhaps challenge what is recorded is obvious. If you have ever had the chance to read a report written about yourself – perhaps as a testimonial or reference – these points will resonate with you.

The opportunity to challenge such reports is recognized, though in the case of job references it can lead to a blandness which at one level says very little even if the practised reader can detect (unfavourable) coded messages.

But if the ethnographic account is seen as a partnership then the checking function serves a different purpose. Whyte (1993, p. 341), as so often, provides a model in this instance:

> As I wrote, I showed the various parts to Doc and went over them with him in detail. His criticisms were invaluable in my revision. At times, when I was dealing with him and his gang, he would smile and say: 'This will embarrass me but this is the way it was, so go ahead with it.'

That short quotation demonstrates how this form of consultation deals not only with the ethical dimension, but also the challenge of individual construction that can be levelled at ethnographic accounts particularly in written form.

Intrusive questioning

One of the tacit assumptions current in our society is that people can be asked questions about anything – even the most intimate matters and their most personal feelings. This appears to be a consequence of the kind of intrusive, aggressive journalism, daily portrayed in the media, which seems to have acquired a degree of normalcy.

In my dealings with Ian (see pages 59–61) I have felt that I couldn't interrogate and challenge him, that I should be sensitive to his privacy and that my (research) relationship with him should not be an inquisitorial one. Reading the research reports of Kennedy and Fitzpatrick, and Murdoch and her colleagues (see pages 63–4), and despite their clear concern to do something about the 'problem' of begging, I did feel that they were as determined to get their research data as a journalist is to get his/her copy. Perhaps I overstate the case but there is something not quite easy there that bears reflection.

No consideration of ethical issues in a particular style of human research can cover all the ground, especially in the restricted scope of one short chapter. What has been discussed here is intended not just to deal with the specifics of the issues considered, but also to raise awareness of the need to be alert to ethical issues that may only be apparent on careful reflection.

10

The Limitations of Observation

In Chapter 8 we considered the role of self-observation as a research method in its own right, particularly direct access to 'internal' events, though these can to some extent be obtained at second-hand, by interview as well as by diary techniques. By such means all aspects of behaviour can be reported; which brings us to the contrary point that large areas of human activity cannot be witnessed. These include the more mundane aspects of our domestic existence (except where there is a 'live-in' researcher, as Whyte was early in his research project). But such areas as domestic violence, intimate personal confidences and sexual behaviour are almost inaccessible except through interview or questionnaire methods. And even here, it is only comparatively recently that these topics have been systematically researched. The first comprehensive investigation of sexual behaviour in the UK was published as recently as 1994, a project vigorously opposed at the funding stage by the then Prime Minister, Margaret Thatcher, as an intrusion into personal privacy (Johnson *et al.*, 1994).

The evolution of behaviour in its cultural context

But perhaps the greatest limitation of observation, which cannot be made up for by other concurrent methods (i.e. at the same point in time), is the evolution or history of the behaviour and context observed. How did it arise?

How we behave is part of our current social system – our relationships with other people, the roles we inhabit, the norms and expectations of the 'local' culture. So how we are is as much maintained in the present as caused by events in the past. But our personality, the way in which we characteristically behave, has a history within which many of these elements originated. Any complete understanding of the present has to take account of the past; more than that we are part of an *evolving* system. This dimension may not be apparent from brief observation; indeed, may only emerge over a period of time.

So there is a need to consider the *origins* of what one observes and the process of change over time, particularly how these changes come about. Even when someone appears to be 'always the same' – like Ian the Glasgow street beggar – one still has to ask (for adequate understanding): how did he get to that apparently unchanging state? And what would it take to disrupt it?

The need for complementary research methods

Observation cannot tell the whole story; and even when extended over time it can only incorporate a narrow section of the evolution of a group, a culture, or an individual. Of course, what you hear or are told will often have a bearing on, or elucidate, the past. Something like a biographical approach may be required: every culture, every institution, like every individual has a history. What was this community (school, prison, company – or whatever) like twenty, thirty, forty years ago? What is the continuity? What has led to improvement (or decay)? What maintenance factors have been constant?

In the 'cultures' of large, established organizations –

hospitals, schools, courts of law, social work services, for example – there will be extensive documentation of the formal kind: policy documents, regulations, reports, minutes of meetings and so on, but these are only one perspective on the past. Their 'official' character, often a rather self-conscious one, will not display the informal realities which make up the origin of most of what one finds from current observation.

At best such documents are going to require interpretation in the light of the experiences of the doctors and nurses, the teachers, the social workers who have to operate the services represented in this way. Their experiences are likely to be unrecorded in any systematic fashion and it is here that 'life history' interviewing is a possible complementary method (see Gillham, 2005, Chapter 7). Multiple individual interviews are probably the only way to build up the background picture to what is observed in the present. Formal documentation has, at best, to be interpreted and translated by those to whom it presumably relates; and it may, in fact, have had no active relationship at all. This is the dilemma for social historians – how to construct a picture of the social reality which runs alongside what has been documented.

'Interviewing' of one kind or another is often concurrent with observation even if the questions asked are limited and fragmentary. Taylor (1993) made a point of interviewing the women drug users she had been studying at the end of her investigation when she knew what she needed (additionally) to find out; and what would only be uncovered in that more systematic way. And the women involved were only likely to be willing to be interviewed once Taylor had established herself with the group and become trusted over time.

The contribution of observation to theory

Ethnographic studies do not usually adopt a theoretical perspective. This is partly because of the strong emphasis on *description* and the often explicit attempt not to impose an explanation (theory) on what is observed, but to interpret after the event.

This stance is similar to what Glaser and Strauss (1967) describe as *grounded theory*, where explanation emerges from the evidence uncovered. But here we have a conundrum: *what determines the selection of observed elements?* Is there no prior intuitive 'theory' there? Scientists traditionally work from a base of existing theory on the principle that how else would one know what to look for?

In real-world social research the answer is that the motivation of the researcher has to be in terms of human *values*: those aspects of human existence which most people would agree to be of importance. Indeed much of the appeal of social research is precisely because its applications (and content) do reflect human concerns about individuals and social issues.

Our concern to do something about society's ills – the difficulties of the disabled, of single mothers, of the homeless, or the unemployed, of those who are 'antisocial' or illicit drug-dependent – presents us with the challenge of understanding. And this is where appreciative research may have a contribution to make to social action, by developing from that perspective explanations (theories) different from those implicit in the shorthand judgements of those who are more advantaged (but sometimes feel threatened). Taylor provides a good example of this in her study of female drug users: that their 'criminal' activities were an inevitable consequence of their need to fund their drug habit – and where regulated drug provision would have removed the need for shoplifting and prostitution. This is not a new argument, but her detailed account makes the case much better than any

Westly, W. (1970) Violence and the Police: A Sociological Study of Law, Custom and Morality. Cambridge, Mass.: MIT Press.

*Whyte, R. F. (1993), *Street Corner Society* (4th edn). Chicago: University of Chicago Press.

Wright, T. (1990), *The Photography Handbook*. London: Routledge.

* = recommended further reading

Index

academic papers 82, 86
access 42–3
action research 6
ageing 20
Agnew, K. 84
alternate sampling 14–15, 18
anecdotes 76
anonymity 69
approved schools 50
audio-recording 47

begging 10, 54, 55ff, 71, 75, 78
    donations 58
    donors 12, 58, 78
    income 59
    lifestyle 64
    location 56
    resettlement 69
    styles 64
behaviour 2, 36
and observation 69
biographical approaches 100
Brewer, J. and Hunter, A. 7
Bruner, J. 76
Burgess, R. G. 39, 43, 46

case studies 6, 41–2
categories, definition 13, 77
child safety 31
chronological structure 77, 86
closed setting 93

comparison groups 33
Conan Doyle, A. 87
consent 92, 96
constructivism 49, 76ff, 83, 96, 97
content analysis 77
context, psychological 21, 37
control groups 30, 37
Cornerville 48, 49
corrective feedback 25
creative process 83
creativity 83–4
criminal behaviour 96
Crisis 63, 64

data
    collection 4, 41, 47, 69, 85ff
    recording 85
    selection/reduction 77, 87,
        102
Data Protection Act 92
demography 20
demonstration 25
dependent/outcome variables 34
designers 22
Devine, T. 56
diaries/journals 85
digital revolution 69
disability 20, 23
Ditton, J. 47
documents 101
drug users 51ff, 96, 101, 102
dycem 21

ecological psychology 20
ecology 20
empirical research 29
Endnote 27
environment, psychological 21
ethics 69, 91ff
ethnographers 41ff, 67ff
ethnographic collaboration 78
ethnographic report 97
ethnography 3, 39ff
European Union 34, 92
evaluative research 32
event sampling 10ff
exclusive design 22
experimental groups 30
experimental settings 31
experiments 6, 29ff, 37, 49
eye cameras 73

fixations, visual 73
Flanders, N. 9
Ford *Focus* 22
Foucault, M. 91
frame grammar 76

gangs 43, 45, 47, 50
Geertz, C. 45
gender 36
Ghiselin, B. 83
Gillham, B. 7, 15, 101
Gillham, B. and McGilp, H. 83
Glaser, B. G. and Strauss, A. L. 102, 103
Greene, G. 66
grounded theory 102

handedness 22
'helping hand' 21
Hemingway, E. 87
Hitchcock, A. 91
Holdaway, S. T. 39, 94ff
Hugo, V. 87
hypothesis testing 44

Ian 12, 57ff, 71ff, 93, 98, 100
image domination 65

images 69ff
    and meaning 71ff
inclusive design 22
independent living 20
InDesign 88
informal groupings 46
interaction categories 10
interactive communication 78
interpretation 4, 45, 77
interval sampling 14ff
inter-subjectivity 68
interviews 2, 4, 5, 7, 25ff, 41, 53, 64, 76, 96, 99
    life history 101
    training 81ff
intrusion 69, 98
investigative procedures 86

Johnson, A. M. *et al.* 99
John-Steiner, V. 86
journalism 86

Kennedy, C. and Fitzpatrick, S. 63, 64, 98
key informants 41, 52–3

languages (spoken/written)
    abstract functions 35, 70, 88
    alphabetic 35
    Chinese 35
    logographic 35
    pictographic 34
    primitive 34
    written 35
linguistics 76
literature review 8, 44, 49
literature search 7, 59, 61
logbooks 85
logograms/logos 35
Lowell, A. 83

MacDougall, D. 71
Mann, T. 86
Maugham, S. 87
Mead, G. H. 68
meaning, as an attribute 74

Medawar, P. 82
medical science 29
mental experience 81
mental images 68
Merton, H. 44
mirrors, as representation 66
mobility 20
multi-cultural, definition 40
multi-media 65, 67
Murdoch, A. 63, 64

narrative 13, 71, 75ff, 86ff

objectivity 76, 81, 83, 90
observation
    checklist 26
    classroom 9
    covert 40, 93
    detached 9
    experimental 13
    exploratory 6
    insider 39, 48, 89
    in training 24
    non-participant 3, 5, 9, 39
    of self 81ff
    open 23
    outsider 42
    overt 46, 93
    participant 5, 39ff, 50, 68
    preliminary 6
    schedule 10
    selection/reconstruction 66ff
    semi-structured 19ff, 37
    structured 3, 4, 5, 9, 10, 19, 37
    unstructured 3, 5, 10, 19, 39ff
occupational therapy 20, 23
open setting 93
Orwell, G. 91

Patrick, J. 43, 44, 45, 46, 47, 50,
    51, 52, 54
performance analysis 27
photographic sequences 75
photographs, reading of 71ff
photography 60, 65ff, 93
    and reality 66ff

Pink, S. 67, 70, 71
Poincaré, H. 83
police 51, 57, 60, 94
Popper, K. 81
positivism 74
PowerPoint 88
practical experiments 31
pre/post-tests 33, 34
problems of living 2
product manuals 37
psychometrics 74

questionnaires 2, 3, 5, 19
qualitative methods 25
quantitative methods 4, 33

random procedures 30, 34
reality, construction of 67ff
recording
    of data 5, 46, 53, 85–6
    of process 84ff
recording schedule 11
reflective learning 89
reliability 74
representation, visual/verbal 70ff
representational abilities 68
representativeness 14, 15
research methods,
    complementary 100
research procedures 69
research process 48–9, 82ff
research questions 4
research reports 49
research skills 25
risk-taking 54
rough sleeping 57

saccades 73
Saint-Exupéry, A. de 89
sampling 14
    duration 16
    frequency 16
scientific realism 76
scientific research 29, 49
self-constructions 1
self-perception 2

self-reports 1, 81ff
signs/symbols 36
signage systems 34ff
signifier/signified 36, 73ff
Smith, N. C. 56
Smith, Sydney 56
social action 48
social anthropology 40
social exclusion 64
social interaction 49
social organization 41, 49
social relations 49
social research 6
social systems 49, 100
software 27, 33, 88
sponsors 52
street culture 59, 64
sub-cultures 6, 40, 48, 50
sub-dominant hand 22
subjectivity 1, 2, 81
substantive statements 77
surveys 2, 3, 4, 5, 7
symbol systems 68
symbolic interactionism 68

Taylor, A. 44, 50, 52ff, 96, 101, 102
teaching and learning 24ff
television 65–6
testing
  signage systems 36
  significant effects 29, 33
  theory 29, 44

text 69
Thatcher, M. 99
theoretical/atheoretical stance
  44, 102, 103
'thick description' 44–6
time sampling 13, 14ff
triple-blind studies 30
Trollope, A. 87

urban ethnography 54, 60

Vagrancy Act (1837) 56
validity 1, 2, 76, 94
validating sampling 15ff
video-recording 25, 32, 34, 37, 60,
  65, 77, 81
  analysis 8, 32
  demonstration 33
  interpretation 79
  interview 32
visual arts 82
visual depiction 70
visual ethnography 65ff
visual media 65ff
visual, reading of 75
visual reality 65ff
visual representation 65ff

Westley 95
Whyte 40, 41, 42, 43, 44, 47, 48,
  49, 52, 78, 97, 99
work diaries 2